Needlecraft Designs from Our Best Quilts

20 Favorite Quilt Designs Graphed for Needlework

Mary Elizabeth Johnson and Zuelia Ann Hurt

Oxmoor House, Inc., Birmingham

Library of Congress Catalog Card Number: 77-95151
ISBN: 0-8487-0483-5
Manufactured in the United States of America
Sixth Printing 1985

Needlecraft Designs from Our Best Quilts

Book design and interior photography: Steve Logan
Cover design and photography: Robin McDonald
Copying of stitch charts: Elaine Easter
Drawings for needlepoint stitch dictionary: Don Smith
Stitching of projects: Barbara Christopher, Betty Taylor,
Dolly Meshejian, Lynda Bagwell, Tappy Folts
Special thanks to the owners of the quilts who
    graciously provided them for photography: Mrs.
    Mamie Heasly, Mrs. Jewell N. Shores, Mrs.
    Shari Perry; and to the Classic "A" stables and
    the Birmingham Botanical Gardens for
    providing locations.

**All needlecraft charts were designed by
Zuelia Ann Hurt.**

The designers of the individual quilt blocks are listed
underneath their respective quilt blocks on pages
6-10. DMC yarn was used for stitching all the
projects illustrated in this book except the one
shown on the cover. See the instructions for the
individual designs for exact quantities needed.

*An exciting mixture of materials, including Persian
yarn, pearl cotton, and gold and silver threads brings
"Fancy Dresden Plate" to glorious life. The individual
sections are meant to imitate the sumptuous fabrics of
men's ties, from which the original quilt design was often
made. Chart begins on page 56.*

*Illustrated on the title page is detail from "Democrat
Banner," page 24.*

Contents

Introduction

Some of the most consistently appealing designs in our American heritage are our quilt designs. Favored, treasured, savored, and bragged about, quilt designs have formed a tangible link for aesthetics from one generation to the next. The traditional medium for execution of these quilt designs has been fabric, either pieced or appliquéd to form the finished product.

But, great designs are compelling, no matter from what material or by what method they are made. When quilt designs are charted for needlework, the possibilities for application of the design increase tremendously. You can follow a chart to do needlepoint, cross stitch, crewel, pulled thread work, latch hook, black work, white work, mosaics, beadwork, and marquetry as well as patchwork and appliqué. The possibilites for the number of different items you can make also increases, especially the number of small items. Because the designs are on graph paper, you can easily adapt them to canvas as small as 22 mesh for perfect, delicate little quilt motifs, suitable for eyeglass cases, belts, box lids, bell pulls, and the like. But if you use a quick point canvas (about 5 mesh to the inch) you can quickly and easily make larger pieces such as director's chair seats and backs, banners for headboards, floor cushions, even screens. And, of course, you can stitch up a pillow in cross stitch or needlepoint to harmonize with your quilt to add a unique touch!

The quilt designs chosen for charting were taken from three Oxmoor House publications:

Award Winning Quilts, Prize Country Quilts, and *Country Quilt Patterns.* These books are described in detail on the back cover of this book. They contain the patterns for the quilt blocks featured on the next five pages. It is interesting to see and enjoy the original source of the design, and the quilt blocks also offer suggestions for color schemes additional to the ones given with the chart. The charted designs are interpretations of the quilt designs . . . they will not be exactly the same as the quilt block, but it is the difference that makes it interesting to work a favorite motif in a new medium.

The charted designs are planned for different skill levels—beginner, intermediate, and advanced. The skill designation refers to the complexity of the stitches within the design and to the mixture of materials used. If you are at ease with the stitches used in an individual design, then you can work the design. If, however, you are new to needlework, you might begin with a design such as "National Star" which works up quickly and easily. As your confidence and skills grow, you could move on to an intermediate project such as "President's Wreath". When you are comfortable with the intermediate projects, you are ready for an advanced project such as "Fancy Dresden Plate", which utilizes many different stitches and yarns, including gold and silver metallic threads.

We hope that this book will bring you great pleasure as you explore new ways to enjoy these very special and well-loved quilt designs.

"George Washington's Cherry Tree," *shown in work on the cover, is complete here in all its magnificence. A truly regal design, it measures 32" square when worked on 12 mesh canvas. It has been finished into one of a set of two giant floor pillows, and would make an equally fabulous wall hanging.* *Chart begins on page 64.*

The Original Quilt Designs and Their Contributors

"Calico Bouquet", p. 17
Mrs. Mamie Heasley
Little Rock, Arkansas
from *Country Quilt Patterns*

"Bride's Quilt", p. 20
Bessie C. Bowman
Boone's Mill, Virginia
from *Award Winning Quilts*

"Grandma's Square", p. 22
Mrs. C. C. Venable
England, Arkansas
from *Award Winning Quilts*

"Democrat Banner", p. 24
Mary A. Cole
Columbia, Kentucky
from *Award Winning Quilts*

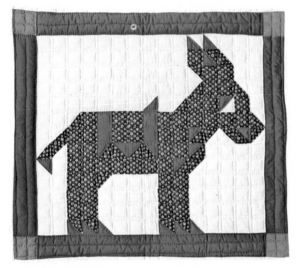

"Donkey", p. 27
Mrs. Jewel G. Jones
Bryan, Texas
from *Country Quilt Patterns*

"New York Beauty", p. 30
Ruth K. Palmer
Niota, Tennessee
from *Award Winning Quilts*

"Rural Background", p. 32
Mrs. Ben F. Harris
Woodland, Alabama
from *Prize Country Quilts*

"President's Wreath", p. 35
Mrs. Annie Linder
Eastview, Kentucky
from *Award Winning Quilts*

"Grandma's Zinnia Basket", p. 38
Ruby Magness
Jennie, Arkansas
from *Award Winning Quilts*

"Tulip", p. 40
Edith S. Longmire
Andersonville, Tennessee
from *Award Winning Quilts*

"Pineapple", p. 42
Mrs. George Steed
Lineville, Alabama
from *Award Winning Quilts*

"National Star", p. 44
Gertrude Mitchell
Russell Springs, Kentucky
from *Award Winning Quilts*

"Lindbergh's Night Flight", p 46.
Ruby Magness
Jennie, Arkansas
from *Prize Country Quilts*

"Cotton Patch Treasures", p. 48
Mrs. Donnell Gowey
Seattle, Washington
from *Prize Country Quilts*

"Oriental Bouquets", p. 50
Mrs. Dorsey Zalants
Columbia, South Carolina
from *Award Winning Quilts*

"Birds and Flowers", p. 53
Jamie McCauley Stephenson
LaFayette, Georgia
from *Country Quilt Patterns*

"Fancy Dresden Plate", p. 56
Mrs. Z. E. Cheatham
Evergreen, Virginia
from *Award Winning Quilts*

"Mrs. Feathersome", p. 59
Mrs. Ray Kimbrell
Warren, Arkansas
from *Prize Country Quilts*

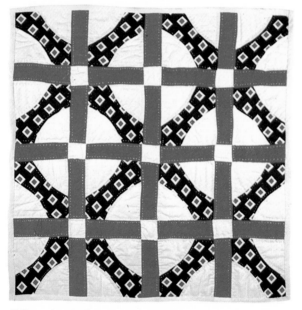

"Grandma's Favorite", p. 62
Annie McGukin
Starr, South Carolina
from *Prize Country Quilts*

"George Washington's Cherry Tree", p. 64
Jewell Shores
Plant City, Florida
from *Prize Country Quilts*

"Donkey" *is sure to please youngsters, especially when he's made into a shaped pillow-pal to play and sleep with. And when you add a set of cross-stitched blocks that spell out his name, you've won someone's heart—a someone who will remember this enchanting design forever. Chart begins on page 27.*

Color Planning and Pattern Placement

Color is the element in any design that makes it come alive. Each design presented in this book is complete with a proposed color scheme. Further color schemes are suggested in the photographs of the quilt blocks on pages 6–10. However, one of the creative aspects you bring to your needlework is your own sense of color and how it should be used. You will surely want to vary the colors of the designs to suit your own preferences. When you do, you should be aware of some very basic rules of color which help insure success. (Work drawings of some of the designs are used here as illustrations to show how our suggested colors were plotted. You might want to adapt this method of working for yourself—make a photocopy of the graph, then color with your desired scheme before you actually buy your yarn or thread.)

To begin with, a color scheme may be *naturalistic,* that is, taken from nature, or it may be *abstract.* Most often in quilt designs, naturalistic color schemes are applied to representational subject matter, as illustrated here in

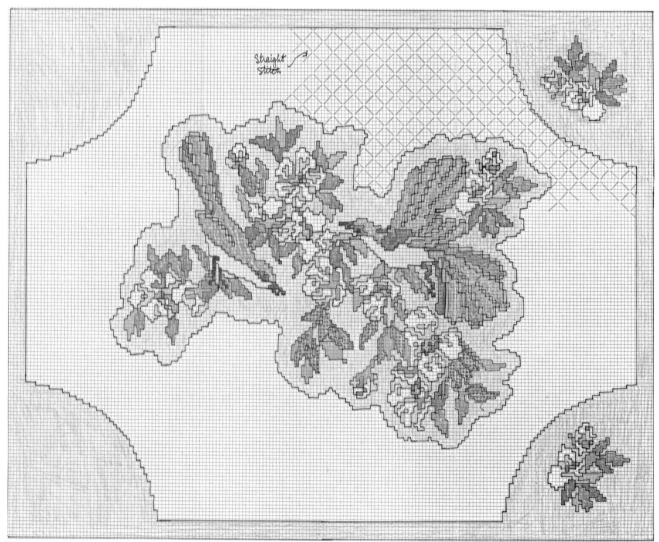

Birds and Flowers

"Birds and Flowers." The greens, blues, and browns of nature are easily recognizable in the plants and birds of the design. An unrealistic or unnatural color scheme for this design would detract from its overall beauty and would inspire a somewhat unsettling feeling.

"Lindbergh's Night Flight" is another example of a realistic color scheme. The plane is a metallic gray, and it is set against a sky that grows deeper and darker as Lindbergh's fabled journey progresses from one square to the next, further across the Atlantic. In this case, the naturalistic color scheme contributes to a feeling of story-like drama.

A successful abstract color scheme has its beginnings in a careful study of a color wheel. A diagram of a color wheel is shown here to help you understand how color schemes work. One of the most common color schemes is a *monochromatic,* or "one-color" scheme.

Pineapple

"Pineapple" is a good example of a color scheme of this type: it uses pale yellow, medium yellow, dark yellow, and brown, which is what yellow becomes when it is darkened to its deepest value.

Another popular color scheme is the *related* scheme, which makes use of colors that are next to one another on the color wheel. "New York Beauty" is a perfect example—the predominant colors are red (crimson), red-orange, and dark brown, which is a very dark orange.

A *complementary* color scheme is one which pairs colors opposite one another on the color wheel. Red and green are opposite one another and work well together all the time, not just at Christmas! "George Washington's Cherry Tree," on the cover and on page 4, is a good example. So is "Cotton Patch Treasures," shown here. "Cotton Patch Treasures" is a complementary color scheme in which the

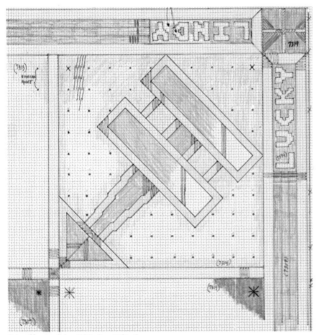

Lindbergh's Night Flight

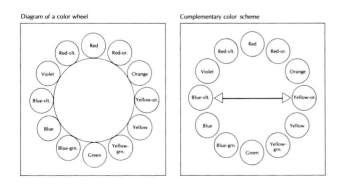

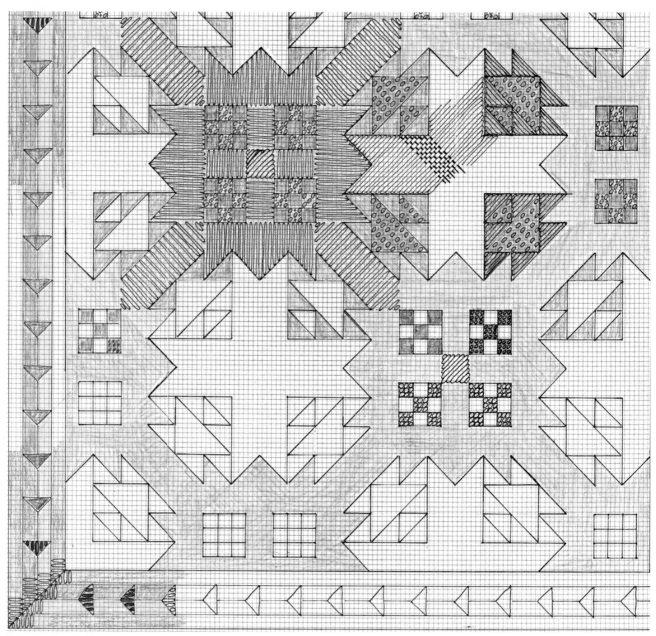

Cotton Patch Treasures

basic colors are muted and worked with two neutrals, white and brown, to achieve a quiet, restful feeling. And, you can use two sets of complements in one color plan, as illustrated in "Tulip." The complementary pairs of blue/orange and yellow/violet are pleasingly combined for a lively, bright effect.

There are many other color schemes that will work well. One is the *triadic* scheme, which utilizes three colors that are the same distance apart on the color wheel. Another is the *ac-cented neutral*, which is what it sounds like—a neutral, such as white, black , navy, accented with a brighter color such as red, yellow, or green. The color schemes discussed here are some of the more basic ones—as you study and learn about color, you will find yourself becoming interested in more and more sophisticated and challenging color arrangements. And that's the fun of working with designs such as these rather than kits—you can choose exactly the colors that please you!

14

How to Repeat a Motif

One of the fascinating things about quilt designs is that most of them are based on a unit (usually a square) that is infinitely repeatable. Thus a project can be made to almost any size desired, if you know in advance the size that each unit will be when it is worked up and the number of times it must be repeated to reach the desired size.

Some designs are made of open-ended units. They can be repeated again and again so that the effect becomes rather like that of a large piece of fabric. Examples of this kind of design are "Pineapple," "New York Beauty," "Cotton Patch Treasures," "Grandma's Square," and "Grandma's Favorite." It is easy to compare the basic unit in this type of design to a brick—you just keep lining them up and stacking them up till you get to the height and width you want. It is, however, a good idea to leave room around the outer edges for a border, to give a nicely finished effect.

Other designs repeat well, but the repeat must be planned carefully before the project is begun. The basic unit in this type of design is rather complex in itself, and can be used alone quite effectively. Examples are: "Lindbergh's Night Flight," "Oriental Bouquets," "President's Wreath," "Calico Bouquet," "Tulip," "Democrat Banner," "National Star," and "George Washington's Cherry Tree." You must decide when planning the project exactly how you want the units to set up—will they work best when carefully placed on a plain background, or do they benefit from dividing strips which act as frames around the individual units? Your decision will, of course, determine the overall size of the finished project and the number of units you will need.

Tulip

A third type of design really works best as a single unit—it does not benefit from repetition, but takes intricate borders with grace and style. These designs are most often realistic interpretations of some scene or creature. "Birds and Flowers," "Rural Background," and "Mrs. Feathersome" are good examples. You can enjoy this type of design best when worked into pillow tops, banners, tote bags, and other items that are good vehicles for displaying a single, striking motif.

Remember also that you can select only a portion of a design if that suits your purposes. An excellent example of a design that offers rich material for "excerpting" is "Democrat Banner"—as you will see when you read the suggestions for projects that accompany the design. Another good design for this purpose is "Grandma's Square," as is "Calico Bouquet."

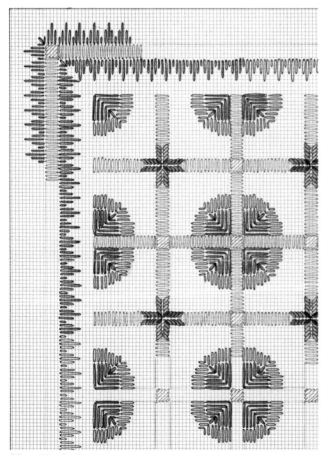

New York Beauty

15

Calico Bouquet
Intermediate Skill Level

All of the colors of springtime are used to stitch roses, daisies, morning glories and chrysanthemums in small and large gingham baskets.

The octagonal shape of the design can be used for either needlepoint or counted cross stitch embroidery. Repeat the chart several times to make larger projects or, lift out individual units of the design and use them as separate charts.

In needlepoint, the design can be worked without the background stitches or with filling in all or part of the background areas.

Projects:

On 14 mesh canvas the octagonal design measures approximately 20" in diameter. On page 16 see it dramatically combined with its coordinating quilt. To make a perfect bedside rug, repeat the full design twice, side by side, and fill in the triangular space on each long side with another small basket so that these sides are straight and only the ends are shaped. Fringe can be added to the shaped ends to match the white, blue or green background colors. Make smaller projects, such as pillows, from the center unit of four small baskets, or a triangular unit, or, place two large basket units side by side with a triangle unit filling in the top and bottom spaces to form a six-sided pillow. The blue/green border or fringe can finish any of these. For a novelty shaped pillow, stitch one of the large baskets and flowers in your choice of color.

Interesting mixed-media projects can be created by working selected areas of the design in cross stitch on an even-weave fabric comparable in the scale of its weave to the canvas gauge, such as 10 mesh canvas plus 11 to-the-inch Aida or a 24 mesh canvas and Aida. The embroidered fabric unit is then appliquéd into its place on the needlepoint canvas.

And, of course, you can stitch your projects entirely in cross stitch if you prefer. Try embroidered placemats with a single flower basket or a tablecloth bordered in alternating sizes of baskets.

Materials:

Persian-type or tapestry wool yarns can be combined with selected colors in pearl cotton when the project is not a rug or table linens.

When part or all of the background is left unworked on canvas, use only a regular mono, otherwise, use a mono interlock canvas.

For cross stitch use an even-weave Aida fabric in white or pastel shades or a tiny pastel gingham check fabric. Use the same yarns as suggested for needlepoint or all pearl cotton, 6-strand cotton floss or a linen floss when making table linens.

For the pillow shown on page 16, we used the following materials:
• 14 mesh non-interlock canvas
• DMC Tapestry wool in the following colors and quantities:
    Color 7110: oxblood—3 skeins (27 yards)
    Color 7107: dark rose—2 skeins (18 yards)
    Color 7104: medium coral—1 skein (9 yards)
    Color 7106: deep coral—1 skein (9 yards)
    Color 7896: pale lilac—1 skein (9 yards)
    Color 7468: brown—4 skeins (36 yards)
    Color 7342: bright chartreuse—1 skein (9 yards)
    Color 7912: light green—3 skeins (27 yards)
    Color 7769: light olive green—2 skeins (18 yards)
    Color 7943: medium green—10 skeins (90 yards)
    Color 7318: dark blue—1 skein (9 yards)
    Color 7316: gray blue—6 skeins (54 yards)
    Color 7314: medium blue—12 skeins (108 yards)
• DMC Pearl Cotton Embroidery Thread, size 3
    Color 740: orange—2 skeins (33 yards)
    Color 310: black—1 skein (16½ yards)
    White: 3 skeins (50 yards)
    Color 444: bright yellow—2 skeins (33 yards)
    Color 552: deep lilac—1 skein (16½ yards)

Gingham baskets filled with calico flowers make "Calico Bouquet" a lively and colorful design that has endless possibilities for stitchery projects. This needlepoint pillow has portions of the background unworked, which makes completion of a project easier and adds to the airy, bright effect. Note that each bouquet is different, which makes for interesting stitching.

Needlepoint stitches:

Tent—Basketweave or continental (to work all bouquets and baskets, large and small)
Brick (background for centered green square and outer blue triangles)
Florentine (for blue and green border rows)

Work order:

Refer to design chart for placement of motifs and mark your canvas into squares and triangles with basting. Put canvas on a frame to work design.

Begin with the small bouquets and baskets in the large center square. Fill background of the center square. Work outer small bouquets and baskets, then fill in triangles with background stitch. Work the large bouquets and baskets. Leave background of these four outer squares unworked. Finish outer edges with a double row of border stitch.

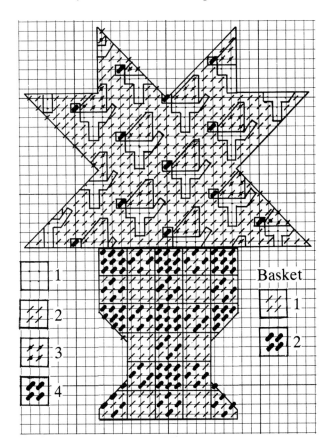

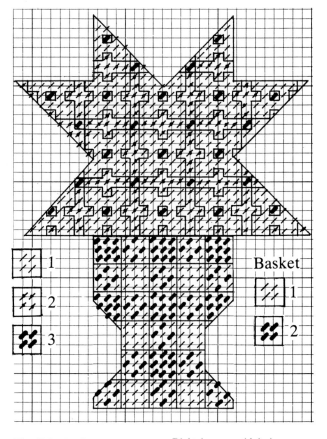

Right Triangle (rose)
1. light green wool
2. brown wool
3. white pearl cotton
4. black pearl cotton
Basket—1. white 2. green
Background: blue

Left Triangle (rose)
1. light green wool
2. brown wool
3. dark rose wool
4. black pearl cotton
Basket—1. white 2. green
Background: blue

Middle
Top bouquet (rose)
1. light green wool
2. bright yellow pearl cotton
3. pale lilac wool
4. black pearl cotton
Basket—1. white 2. blue
Background: green
Bottom bouquet (rose)
1. light green wool
2. bright yellow pearl cotton
3. deep coral wool
4. black pearl cotton
Basket—1. white 2. blue
Background: green

Top Triangle (daisy)
1. gray blue wool
2. brown wool
3. black pearl cotton
Basket—1. white 2. green
Background: blue

Bottom Triangle (daisy)
1. bright yellow pearl cotton
2. brown wool
3. black pearl cotton
Basket—1. white 2. green
Background: blue

Right bouquet (daisy)
1. deep coral wool
2. bright yellow pearl cotton
3. black pearl cotton
Basket—1. white 2. blue
Background: green

Left bouquet (daisy)
1. orange pearl cotton
2. bright yellow pearl cotton
3. black pearl cotton
Basket—1. white 2. blue
Background: green

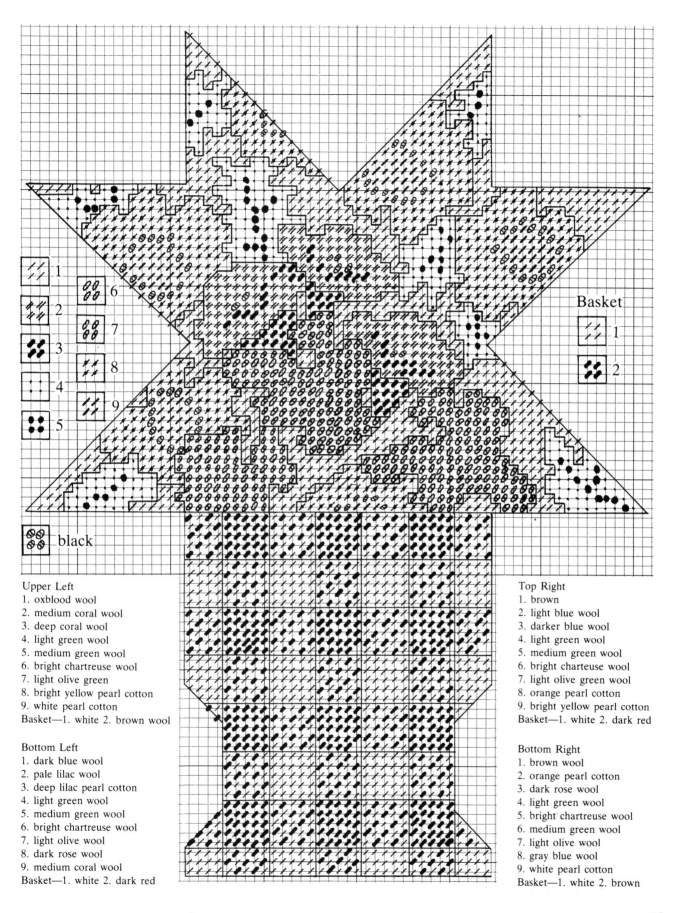

Basket

black

Upper Left
1. oxblood wool
2. medium coral wool
3. deep coral wool
4. light green wool
5. medium green wool
6. bright chartreuse wool
7. light olive green
8. bright yellow pearl cotton
9. white pearl cotton
Basket—1. white 2. brown wool

Bottom Left
1. dark blue wool
2. pale lilac wool
3. deep lilac pearl cotton
4. light green wool
5. medium green wool
6. bright chartreuse wool
7. light olive wool
8. dark rose wool
9. medium coral wool
Basket—1. white 2. dark red

Top Right
1. brown
2. light blue wool
3. darker blue wool
4. light green wool
5. medium green wool
6. bright chartreuse wool
7. light olive green wool
8. orange pearl cotton
9. bright yellow pearl cotton
Basket—1. white 2. dark red

Bottom Right
1. brown wool
2. orange pearl cotton
3. dark rose wool
4. light green wool
5. bright chartreuse wool
6. medium green wool
7. light olive wool
8. gray blue wool
9. white pearl cotton
Basket—1. white 2. brown

Bride's Quilt
Beginner Skill Level

The bright red, yellow and green colors and the heart shapes in this design suggest that it easily could have originated in the Pennsylvania Dutch countryside as a stencil pattern. The simple stitches accentuate this feeling.

As a needlepoint project consider leaving the background unworked so that the white canvas becomes an open airy background for the stitches.

Projects:

On 12 mesh canvas the design measures 13½" square without the border. With the border, the design measures 14¾" square on 12 mesh canvas. Work the entire design with background for a square pillow. Use only the wreath of leaves and the four center hearts as the design within a heart-shaped pillow and add an eyelet or lace ruffle around the edge.

Materials:

When filling the background with stitches use a mono interlock canvas; if you are omitting background stitches use a regular mono canvas. Persian-type wool yarn is suggested.

Needlepoint Stitches:

Byzantine (hearts, worked in alternate directions)
Cross (background)
Straight (leaves and border)
Tent—Continental (stem and border) and Basketweave (border)

Work Order

Start at the center and work the top half of the design first, then the lower half.

If you are making a heart-shaped pillow, work the wreath and center hearts. Then place tracing paper over the worked area and draw one side of a heart large enough to include half the needlepoint plus some space. Draw a center line and then fold the paper on this line and draw the second half of the heart. Center and pin the paper heart on top of the needlepoint. Pin a white or colored fabric liner to the wrong side and machine stitch around the heart shape through paper, canvas and fabric. Remove the paper, add the eyelet or lace ruffle and then finish constructing the pillow.

white
yellow
red
green
brown

Grandma's Square
Advanced Skill Level

Grandma definitely had a flare for the dramatic when she arranged colors and patterns within this simple square shape. Colors flow from dark to light to dark again, whether in solids or prints.

The needlepoint design contains ten different tent stitch patterns, one mosaic pattern repeated in seven colors and a black and white checkerboard border.

Projects:

Each needlepoint square or pattern uses 18 meshes in each direction. Therefore, on 18 mesh canvas the entire design produces a 17¾" square project. Multiples of the design without the border can be used to produce impressive needlepoint upholstery for the back and seat of a wing chair. In this case, units #11—#17 should be changed to the basket weave stitch.

The stitch patterns can be rearranged or lifted out of the chart to make a variety of projects, such as picture or mirror frames, pillows, tote or evening bags, or a belt. The belt could use the horizontal center row from the chart with unit #1 at the center back and units #1—#10 repeated toward each end for the needed length. When the border is added around all sides the belt would measure 1¾" wide on 18 mesh canvas.

Materials:

For upholstery use only a wool yarn and an interlock mono or penelope canvas. A creative mixture of yarns can be used on most other projects. Combine wool with pearl cotton or 6-strand cotton floss for selected colors to imitate the luster of brocades and silks.

The design is most effective on petit point canvas gauges.

Needlepoint Stitches:

Mosaic (alternating direction for border; optional, units #11—#17.)
Straight (optional, as embroidery on top of needlepoint between units #11—#17.)
Tent—Continental and Basketweave (worked in one and two colors)

Work Order:

Use a permanent ink marking pen to mark off the canvas in 18 mesh squares. Start at the upper left corner and work the squares in horizontal rows. Add the border last.

To finish the edges of a belt or frame, work all the pattern squares and any border. Then finish the edges.

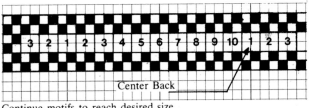

Continue motifs to reach desired size.

Note: Work the left and right positions of motif #2 as *horizontal* stripes and work the top and bottom positions as *vertical* stripes.

Each numbered square in the diagram represents a motif that spans 18 meshes by 18 meshes.

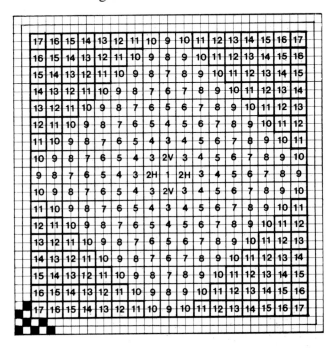

17	16	15	14	13	12	11	10	9	10	11	12	13	14	15	16	17
16	15	14	13	12	11	10	9	8	9	10	11	12	13	14	15	16
15	14	13	12	11	10	9	8	7	8	9	10	11	12	13	14	15
14	13	12	11	10	9	8	7	6	7	8	9	10	11	12	13	14
13	12	11	10	9	8	7	6	5	6	7	8	9	10	11	12	13
12	11	10	9	8	7	6	5	4	5	6	7	8	9	10	11	12
11	10	9	8	7	6	5	4	3	4	5	6	7	8	9	10	11
10	9	8	7	6	5	4	3	2V	3	4	5	6	7	8	9	10
9	8	7	6	5	4	3	2H	1	2H	3	4	5	6	7	8	9
10	9	8	7	6	5	4	3	2V	3	4	5	6	7	8	9	10
11	10	9	8	7	6	5	4	3	4	5	6	7	8	9	10	11
12	11	10	9	8	7	6	5	4	5	6	7	8	9	10	11	12
13	12	11	10	9	8	7	6	5	6	7	8	9	10	11	12	13
14	13	12	11	10	9	8	7	6	7	8	9	10	11	12	13	14
15	14	13	12	11	10	9	8	7	8	9	10	11	12	13	14	15
16	15	14	13	12	11	10	9	8	9	10	11	12	13	14	15	16
17	16	15	14	13	12	11	10	9	10	11	12	13	14	15	16	17

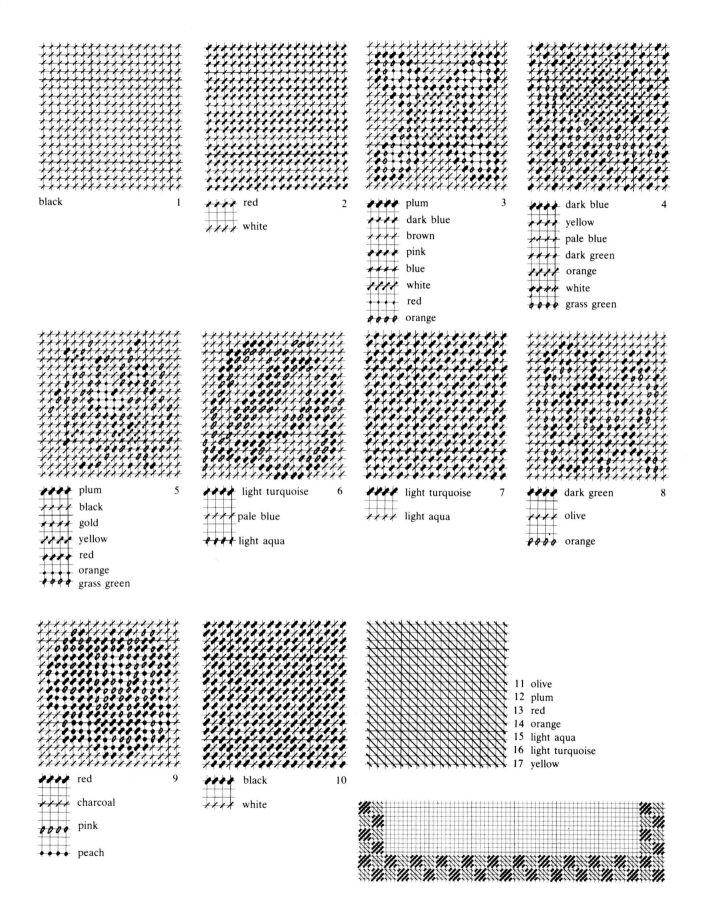

black   1

red
white
    2

plum
dark blue
brown
pink
blue
white
red
orange
    3

dark blue
yellow
pale blue
dark green
orange
white
grass green
    4

plum
black
gold
yellow
red
orange
grass green
    5

light turquoise
pale blue
light aqua
    6

light turquoise
light aqua
    7

dark green
olive
orange
    8

red
charcoal
pink
peach
    9

black
white
    10

11 olive
12 plum
13 red
14 orange
15 light aqua
16 light turquoise
17 yellow

23

Democrat Banner
Advanced Skill Level

The multitude of shapes in this design makes it a very versatile pattern. In addition to using the chart as is, selected areas can be used alone to create an endless variety of separate needle point projects. Even though the design is suited to advanced skills, the beginning needlepointer can use the center area and border for easy quick projects.

Projects:

When the entire design is worked on 14 mesh canvas, a 16" square is produced. The design forms a perfect boxed pillow when the corner roses are omitted. Knife edge pillows can be made with or without the border of trailing roses. When the rose and buds are omitted from the center space, dates for a wedding or birth sampler or a monogram can be included. Stitch the central area alone for a charming miniature pillow to toss in with one using the full design. Use the border alone to create mirror or picture frames. And, why not use the single corner rose for a pin cushion or sachet?

Materials:

Beginners using areas of the design for quick projects should select larger canvas gauges than suggested above: namely 7, 10 or 12 mesh. Persian-type or tapestry wool yarns are suggested.

Needlepoint Stitches:

Backstitch or Stem (to outline areas)
Cross (two-color stitch for center and border backgrounds)
Oriental (four-color stitch)
Slanting Encroaching Gobelin
Straight (as embroidery with buds)
Tent—Continental and Basketweave (remaining background)

Work Order:

Mark the border areas on the canvas with basting thread. Proceed to work the design from top to bottom, leaving the backgrounds until last.

The cross stitch is worked in two colors, with the first half of the stitch worked in off-white and the second half on top in yellow yarn. Add the straight stitches to the buds and outline the large corner leaves and the center section last.

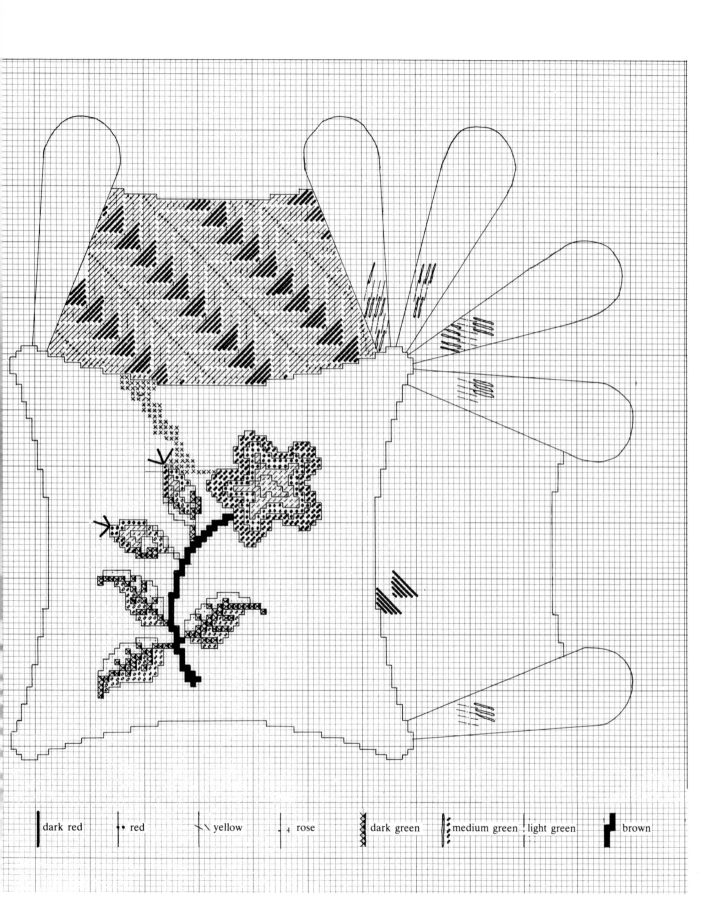

dark red	red	yellow	rose	dark green	medium green	light green	brown

Donkey
Beginner Skill Level

What child would not delight at having this bashful friend as a companion in his or her own room! Children will love him in bright primary colors. Adults will want to adopt him for themselves in dusty antique colors.

He can be made in needlepoint or translated into embroidery on an even-weave fabric.

Projects:

Worked on 12 mesh canvas the design measures 14" by 12½". Several projects are shown on page 11. The fabric quilt has been teamed with a donkey-shaped needlepoint pillow and six soft gingham building blocks that spell out D-O-N-K-E-Y in cross stitched letters. Each letter is framed with two rows of a cross stitch border and worked on only one side of the colorful gingham cube. Make a twin size headboard by arranging two donkeys in a line and placing the border around the outside of the animals so that the word "donkey" appears twice along the top and bottom.

Materials:

Use a mono interlock canvas and Persian-type wool yarn for all needlepoint projects. A 7 mesh canvas was used to make the photographed donkey-shaped pillow, with the yarn doubled in the needle. However, 10 or 12 mesh would work well too. The blocks were embroidered on gingham that has ⅛" squares. Each cube measures approximately 6" in each direction.

For the donkey-shaped pillow, we used the following quantities of DMC 3-ply Persian wool, "Floralia":
Color 7526: brown—10 skeins (55 yards)
Color 7899: blue—2 skeins (11 yards)
Color 7107: red—1 skein (5½ yards)
Color 7434: yellow—1 skein (5½ yards)
White: 1 skein (5½ yards)
Black: 3 skeins (17 yards)
Each cross stitched cube takes approximately 2 skeins (55 yards) of DMC 6-strand cotton embroidery floss.

The entire design can be embroidered on a 14 to-the-inch even-weave Aida fabric with 6-strand cotton floss.

Needlepoint Stitches:
Binding (for donkey-shaped pillow only)
Byzantine (background)
Tent—Continental and Basketweave (letters and their background)
Triangle (with cross stitch in corners, for donkey)
Upright Gobelin (border)

Alternate Stitches for Embroidery:
Triangle (with cross stitch corners, for donkey)
Stem (to outline donkey-shaped pillow only)
Cross (to replace Tent and Upright Gobelin)
(Note: Areas of the design not mentioned above need not be stitched.)

Work Order:

When working the complete design start by marking off the border areas with basting thread. Begin at the top of the border and work down, saving the background (needlepoint) for last.

When working the donkey-shaped pillow, work all of the triangle stitches and then go around the perimeter of the animal with either the binding or the stem stitch. Trim away the excess canvas or fabric so that a ½" seam allowance remains all around. Cut out a back for the pillow using this trimmed front for a pattern. Cut a 2" wide strip in a length to fit completely around donkey for boxing. Make cording twice this length. Sew cording to donkey along seamline, then sew boxing to donkey. Sew remaining cording to free edge of boxing, then sew pillow back to corded edge of boxing, leaving an opening to insert polyester stuffing. Slipstitch opening closed.

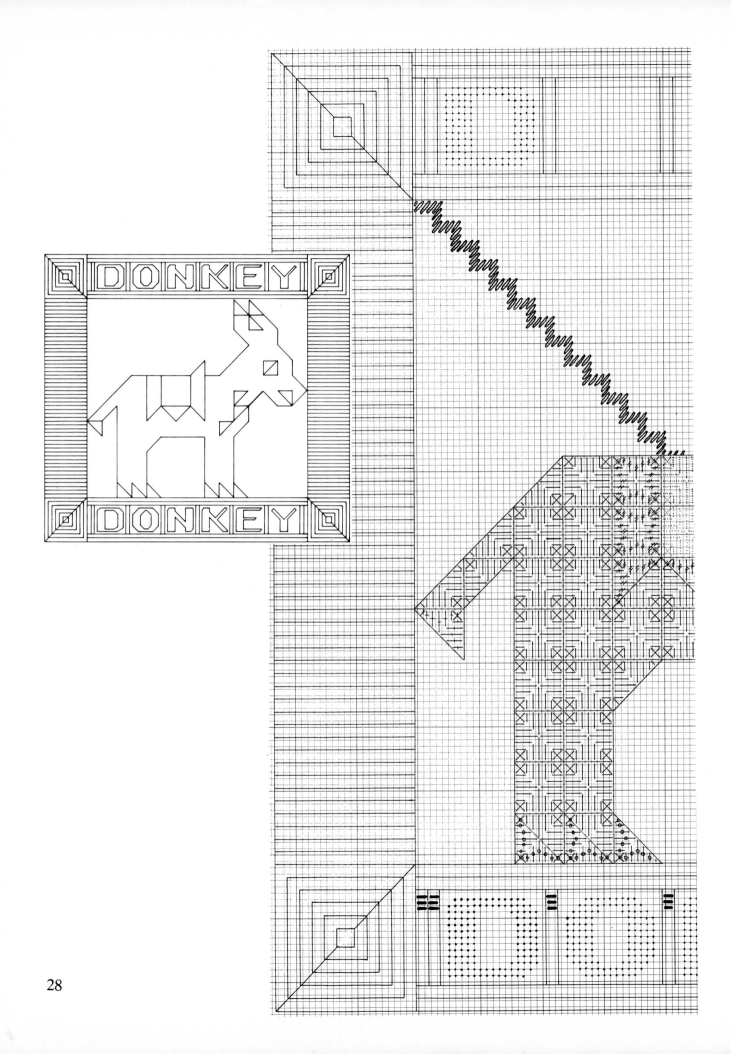

28

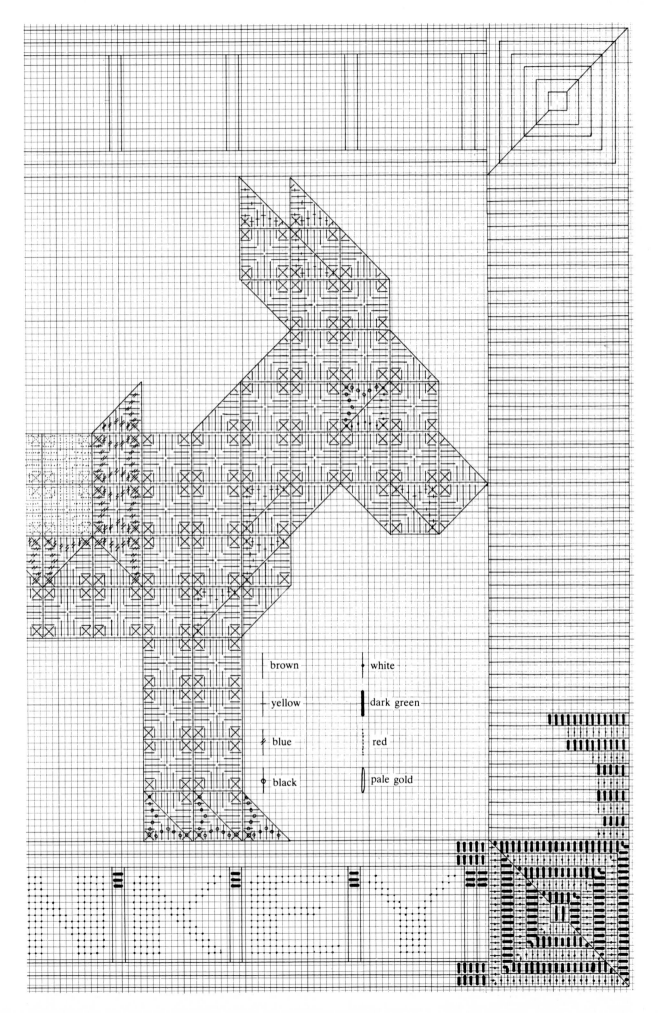

brown		white
yellow		dark green
blue		red
black		pale gold

29

New York Beauty
Intermediate Skill Level

The miniature all-over pattern of this needle-point design is in direct contrast to the giant 31" quilt square which provided the inspiration. Handsome textile coordinates of both the quilt and needlepoint versions would be exciting in almost any type room. The needlepoint repeat can be continued to make a project of any size, square or rectangular in shape.

Projects:

One repeat of the design uses 42 canvas meshes in each direction and includes two vertical and two horizontal cream bands, a quarter circle in each corner and one star. Omit the cream bands around the perimeter of your arrangement, as does the chart. This flexibility of arrangement makes it possible to make pillows, floor cushions, bench or chair cushions of any size. Even needlepoint upholstery is possible when the border is omitted.

Materials:

For upholstery, use a 16 or 18 mesh mono interlock canvas; otherwise, 12 or 14 mesh would be appropriate. Tapestry or Persian-type wool yarns are suggested.

Needlepoint Stitches:

Upright Gobelin (cream bands)
Slanted Encroaching Gobelin or Tent—Basketweave (either for background)
Straight
Mosaic

Work Order:

Work the design in horizontal rows of a repeat depth, then the border, then the background.

When working the border, start at the center of each side and work to the corner. The crimson and scarlet stitches in the border may need compensating corner stitches different from those charted. Each color will always work out evenly on each side of the corner, but the small adjustment is necessary because the number of repeats within each project may vary.

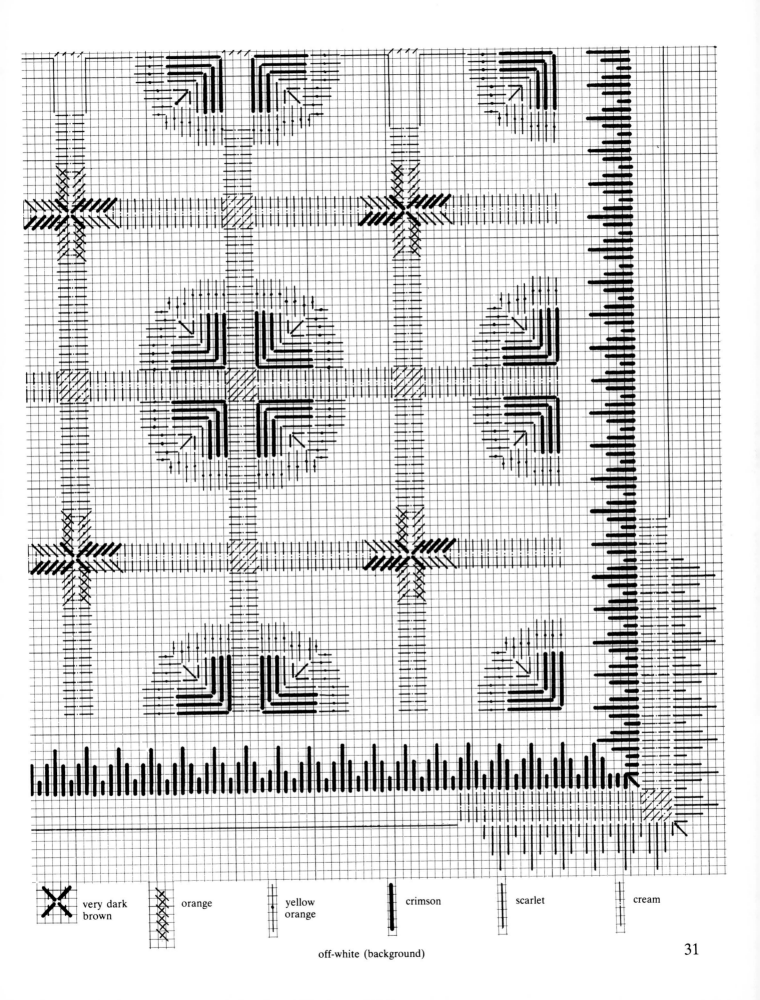

very dark brown

orange

yellow orange

crimson

scarlet

cream

off-white (background)

31

Rural Background
Advanced Skill Level

Vertical satin-like stitches are practically the only stitches used to compose this serene rural scene designed for needlepoint. Details and color changes keep the work interesting and challenging even though the finished effect looks simple.

Projects:

On 12 mesh canvas the design measures approximately 15¾" square. To make a wall hanging, include four 1½" wide tabs across top and purchase or make four fat 3½" long tassels for the bottom edge. Place a lucite or wood rod through the tabs and hang the banner on nails concealed behind the tabs or on a decorative hook. Make a pillow without the tabs and add tassels or fringe to each side. The design also works well as a tote bag.

Materials:

Use Persian-type wool yarn on a mono interlock canvas.

Needlepoint Stitches:

Binding (wall hanging or banner only)
Mosaic (dove's head)
Straight (worked vertically, horizontally and diagonally)
Turkey Knot (optional fringe)

Work Order:

First, mark off the canvas into 64 squares each containing 22 canvas threads in each direction; draw eight across and eight down. Use a fine tip permanent ink marking pen. If needed, also draw the tabs. These lines will help you keep your place in counting the stitches while working. Work the design from top down, except fill in the sun and its rays after the mountain tops and clouds have been worked.

To finish the wall hanging, work the binding stitch around the perimeter in dark cobalt. Trim away canvas to leave a ½" seam allowance. Turn the seam to the back and line the banner with navy felt. Add tassels and fold back the tabs to form loops and tack the ends to the back.

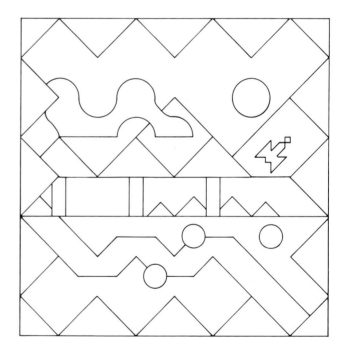

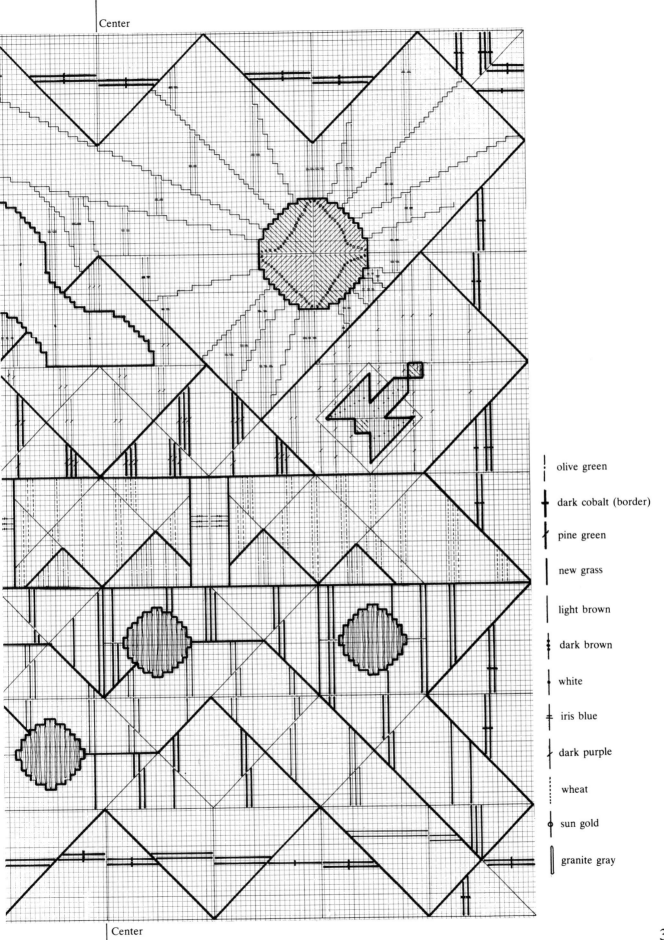

Center

Center

olive green

dark cobalt (border)

pine green

new grass

light brown

dark brown

white

iris blue

dark purple

wheat

sun gold

granite gray

33

President's Wreath
Intermediate Skill Level

A traditional calico pattern for the flowers is placed against a delicate peach background which is stitched to imitate the wreath of flowers and duplicate the quilting lines of its appliquéd quilt predecessor.

The chart presents a choice of shapes, square or round, for various projects in needlepoint or counted cross stitch.

Projects:

On 14 mesh canvas or 14 to-the-inch even-weave cross stitch fabric the finished piece would have a 14" diameter or side, perfect for a set of cross stitch chair cushions or a needlepoint pillow. The design can also be used to make a half-round tea cozy that measures 14" wide by 9" high. Use either canvas, even-weave fabric, or a tiny pastel gingham fabric (the latter for cross stitch). When made in fabric, the design areas of the silhouetted flowers can be quilted.

A square project finishes with a white buttonhole and wine tent stitch (or cross stitch) border; a round project finishes with a round brown border of tent stitches (or cross stitches). The tea cozy has the brown border around the curved and straight edges.

Materials:

For needlepoint, use Persian-type or tapestry wool yarn plus, for an interesting textural contrast, a pearl cotton yarn for the wine and mustard colors which form the flowers in the calico.

For embroidery, use an even-weave Aida fabric in white or pink and 6-strand cotton floss, linen floss or floss plus pearl if the project is to be washed. If the project won't be washed, consider Persian-type wool yarn for the dominant yarn on the fabric.

Needlepoint Stitches:
Brick (background)
Buttonhole (border)
Cross (center of flowers)
Florentine (flower silhouettes)
Straight (eyelet variation, radial center of flowers)
Tent—Continental and Basketweave
Alternative:
Backstitch (to form flower silhouettes for real or fake quilting)
Buttonhole (square projects only)
Cross or Double Cross (replacing Tent)
Straight

Work Order:

For all projects, work one quarter of the wreath at a time. Begin with a round flower and then work the stem and the next flower, then the leaves in between. Next, work the border and background for needlepoint projects.

If you want a quilted background remove the embroidery from the hoop and baste a layer of quilt batting and a backing fabric under the embroidery. Place it back in the hoop and make backstitches.

If you are making a tea cozy, machine stitch around the outside shape next to the border

and trim away the excess fabric to ½" all around. (Add batting and a backing fabric to back of needlepoint before stitching and trimming.) Then cut a back piece for the cozy by using the front as a pattern; cut back batting and backing fabric. Sew the front and back together and finish the lower edge with bias tape that is then hand stitched to the inside.

wine   mustard   brown   green   pale peach

white

coral

Grandma's Zinnia Basket
Intermediate Skill Level

Baskets of brightly colored zinnias are arranged in rows for an all-over pattern framed with a florentine border in straw, chestnut and berry colors. A variation on the eyelet stitch produces a raised texture for the zinnias, complementing the gathered pull flowers in its quilt counterpart.

We suggest the projects be worked on a natural brown mono canvas with the background around the baskets left unworked. The canvas color will blend right in with the earth colors in the baskets and border. Or, if you prefer filling in the background, use the basketweave stitch but use two colors, white and off-white, in alternating rows to make a richer color.

Projects:
On a 13 mesh natural brown mono canvas the design as charted would make a 16" by 17" pillow. Consider coordinating the pillow with a bell pull made with a vertical row of baskets for the desired length and the zig-zag stitches as side borders. The bell pull would measure 5½" wide and fit the standard brass ends. The repeat length is approximately 7½" on 13 mesh canvas.

Materials:
If the background of the design is being left unworked as an element of the design, then select a regular mono canvas so that it will have the appearance of an even-weave fabric. Otherwise, if you are filling in the background, use an interlock canvas. Tapestry wool yarns are favored for a smooth clear surface.

Needlepoint Stitches:
Binding (bell pull only)
Cross
Eyelet (variation as charted)
Florentine (border as charted)
Tent—Continental
Basketweave (optional background, in two yarn colors)

Work Order:
Work all the basket units first—the flowers, then the basket. Then work the zig-zag stitches dividing the baskets and the florentine border, if used. Work the optional white/off-white background last.

To finish the side edges of the bell pull, fold the canvas sides back so that the width measures 5½" and work the binding stitch along the folded edges.

Projects with the background of the canvas left unworked will need a layer of felt or fabric matching the canvas color placed against the wrong side of the stitches before the lining for the bell pull is added or the pillow is constructed.

spruce green   chestnut brown   berry red   straw

gold   red   apricot   white and off-white
(optional for background)

39

Tulip
Beginner Skill Level

Bold areas of color are used to stitch this intriguing sun-ray arrangement of tulips, making a stronger statement than the subtle prints of the original quilt block. The four-way byzantine stitch background in dark brown works well for finishing the project into a round or square shape. Two types of yarn in matching shades are mixed in the weaving stitch to work the flowers, with the backstitch added on top to give petal definition.

Projects:

On 10 mesh mono interlock canvas a project would have an 18" diameter or side. On 12 mesh the size would be 15". Make a round footstool on either of these meshes and, if the stool is larger than the charted area, just continue the background to reach the increased size. A nice finishing touch for pillows would be two or three rows of ruffles in eyelet or lace around the edges, each in a different width.

Materials:

For the flowers, select Persian-type wool yarn and a comparable shade of pearl cotton yarn for each of the four flower colors. Let the darker of the two shades be in the wool. Use the same type of wool for all of the other stitches.

Needlepoint Stitches:

Backstitch (inside flower; optional, to outline flowers)
Byzantine (background)
Double Cross (Upright Cross plus cross in center of design)
Leaf (elongated variation)
Straight (stems)
Weaving (flowers)

Work Order:

Work the four straight stitch stems and then the double leaf stitch stems. Next, work the wool part of each flower, laying the blue and apricot wools vertically and the yellow and lavender wools horizontally. Weave in the pearl yarns on the flowers. Work the four-way background a quarter at a time. Add backstitches on top of the flowers in pearl yarn to match and if desired, around the outside of each flower.

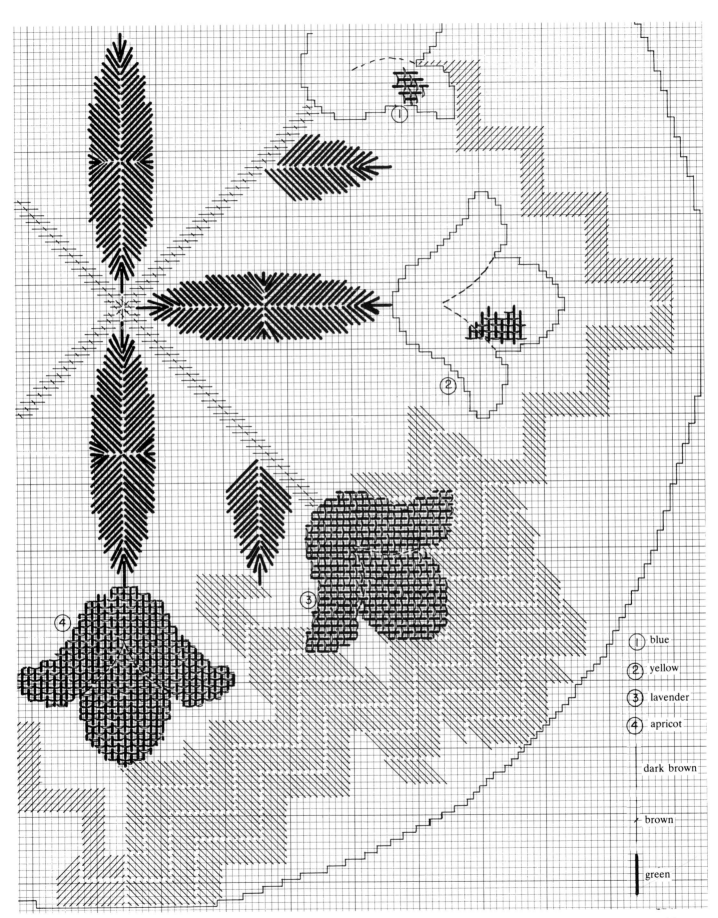

1 blue

2 yellow

3 lavender

4 apricot

dark brown

brown

green

Pineapple
Advanced Skill Level

When worked in the monochromatic yellow-to-brown color family, this design captures the texture and color of the tropical fruit for which it is named. If you elect to go with a free-form color scheme more like the one used in the original quilt block, this is an excellent choice for using up scrap bits of yarn.

The octagonal pattern repeat of this design can be worked in any of three different schemes: first, it can always be worked in tent stitches (basketweave) except for its small eyelet center; second, it can always be worked in upright gobelin stitch (vertically and horizontally) with the center in eyelet stitch; or third, the first two options can be alternated in a checkerboard fashion throughout the project. In any of these options always work the eyelet square dividing the octagons as it is charted. The perimeter spaces between the pattern and the border should be worked in either the slanted encroaching gobelin or basketweave stitch.

The pattern repeat can be continued to produce square or rectangular projects of any size.

Projects:

One repeat of the pattern uses 40 threads of the canvas in each direction and includes one octagonal unit plus two square dividing units. A pillow, cushion, frame, tote bag and bell pull are some of the projects to make with this design. And, since the pineapple is the traditional symbol of hospitality, you'll want to be sure to find a place for this design somewhere in your home, as an interesting variation on the traditional motif.

Materials:

Canvas gauges of 14 mesh or finer will produce the best results. Do use a mono interlock canvas. The design is particularly handsome when wool yarn is used and metallic gold stitches are added on top of the wool eyelet stitches.

Needlepoint Stitches:

Eyelet (as a needlepoint stitch; as embroidery on top of needlepoint)
French Knot (center of each eyelet)
Upright Gobelin
Upright Encroaching Gobelin (optional stitch for background)
Straight (diagonal stitches used with Upright Gobelin)
Tent—Basketweave (optional stitch for background)

Work Order:

Start at the upper left and work the design in horizontal rows of the repeat. Fill in the border and then add the metallic gold embroidery stitches, eight evenly spaced ones, over each eyelet stitch. Add the wool French knots last to the center of each eyelet stitch.

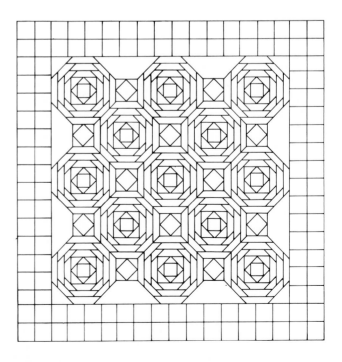

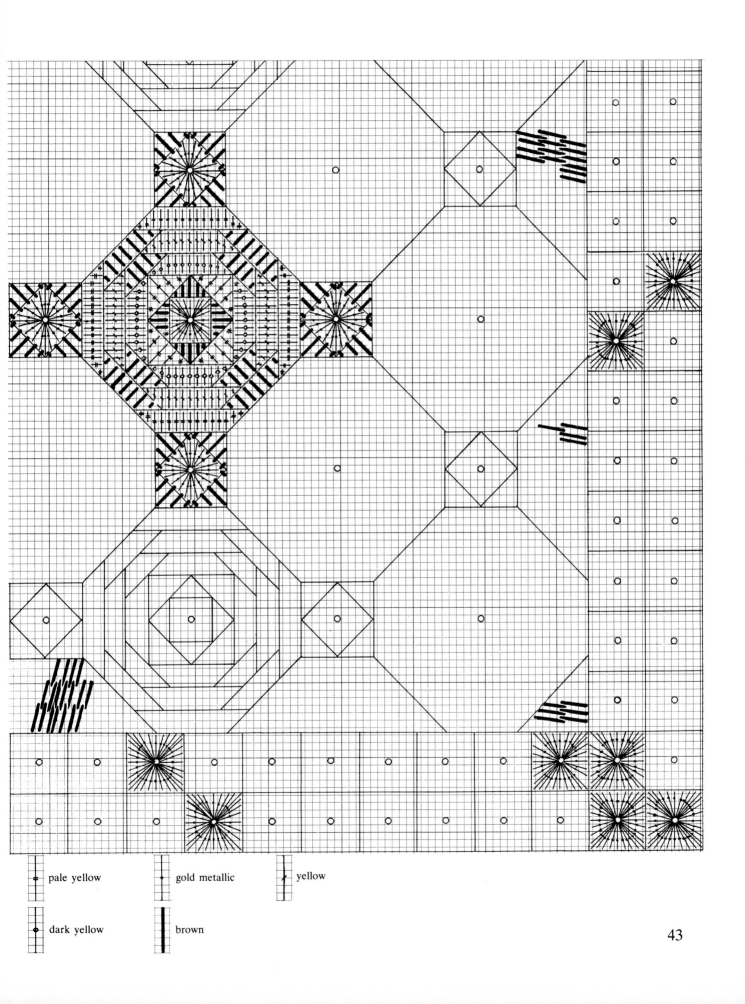

| | pale yellow | | gold metallic | | yellow |
| | dark yellow | | brown | | |

National Star
Beginner Skill Level

This simple design is ideal for a quick beginner's project when worked as a single star motif on a large gauge needlepoint canvas. It is also superb for a latch hook project.

Projects:
For the beginner we suggest a pillow or a wall banner hung with tasseled rope tacked at the top corners stitched either in needlepoint or latch hook.

A single motif with border on a 7 mesh canvas would make a 25½" square project.

Other needlecrafters may want to make a larger project or one on a smaller gauge canvas with multiples of the star, such as a rug or a tote bag.

Materials:
On the 7 mesh canvas Persian-type wool can be used doubled in the needle. If the design is worked in needlepoint, the stripes around the star and in the border can be worked either in tent stitches with yarn or as long straight stitches done in a bulky yarn or a small rayon or rat-tail cord over and under the white tent stitches.

If you select the latch hook technique, use a low pile yarn for the stars and border and a high pile yarn for the background where slanted gobelin stitches are indicated on the chart. A low pile can be used throughout if you switch to a contrasting or an off-white yarn for the background so that the small corner stars will not disappear.

Needlepoint Stitches:
Slanted Gobelin (background, alternating directions per row)
Straight (with canvas grain and on the bias)
Two-way Tent—Continental

Alternative Stitches:
Latch Hook

Work Order:
For needlepoint, start in the center, working one quarter of the large star at a time. Next, work the stripes around the large star and the border. Work the four corner stars and then the background. If cord is being used instead of yarn for the stripes, finish and block the design before inserting the cords.

For latch hook, turn book upside down and work the design one row at a time from left to right and from bottom to top.

44

white   red   blue

Lindberg's Night Flight
Beginner Skill Level

Lindy's airplane is arranged in multiples so that it flies from dusk to dark as the shade of blue yarn used for the background gradually changes. And, of course, the silver stars get bigger and brighter as the depth of night advances. Keep the formation of four as charted or rearrange the bi-planes into a horizontal climb with the words "Lucky Lindy" beside only the lower left and upper right corners of the border.

Projects:

Worked on 12 mesh canvas, the design as charted with four stacked units measures 16½" square. As one unit with a border it measures 10" square; as three horizontally arranged units it measures 24" by 10". The design can be used for pillows, a bench cushion, wall banner or a headboard for a bed.

Materials:

Persian-type wool yarns and mono interlock canvas are suggested. The embroidered stars on the blue backgrounds should be worked in a contrasting yarn such as a silver metallic or a silver shade of 6-strand cotton floss or pearl cotton, #5 size.

Needlepoint Stitches:

Cross (as embroidery for stars)
Double Cross (combination of Upright Cross and Cross as embroidery for stars)
Eyelet (at center of design when units have stacked arrangement)
French Knot (as embroidery for stars)
Upright Gobelin (border)
Mosaic (corner motif)
Slanted Encroaching Gobelin (background)
Straight (bi-planes)
Tent—Continental and Basketweave (border words and background)

Work Order:

Draw the bi-plane units, the dividing borders and outside border lines on the canvas with a fine tip blue permanent ink marking pen. Work the design from top to bottom, filling in the backgrounds and the embroidered stars last. The stars are embroidered every eight canvas threads, first as a French knot, next as a cross stitch over two threads, next as a double cross over two threads and last as a double cross over four canvas threads.

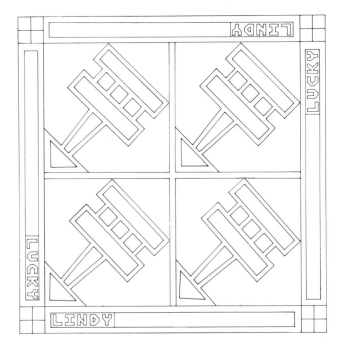

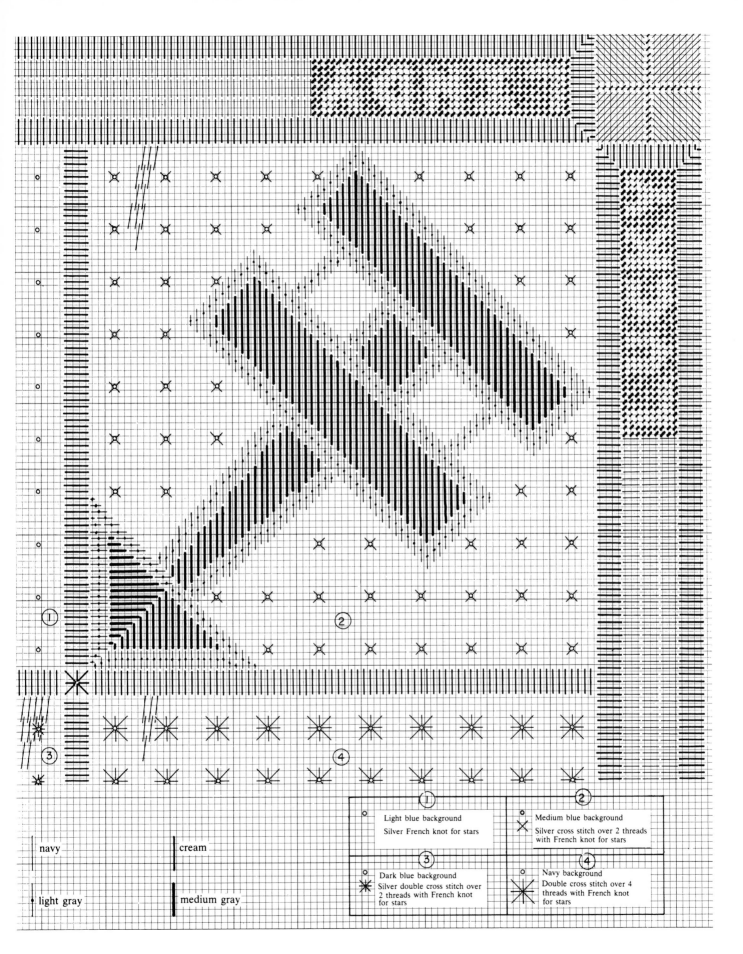

①	
°	Light blue background
	Silver French knot for stars

②	
°	Medium blue background
✕	Silver cross stitch over 2 threads with French knot for stars

③	
°	Dark blue background
✳	Silver double cross stitch over 2 threads with French knot for stars

④	
°	Navy background
✳	Double cross stitch over 4 threads with French knot for stars

navy

cream

light gray

medium gray

Cotton Patch Treasures
Intermediate Skill Level

Chickens, speckled eggs, grass, arrowheads, crosses and crowns are symbolically represented in the design called Cotton Patch Treasures. Rich earth colors are appropriately used in textural stitches that speak of the treasures portrayed. This all-over pattern can be extended to any size for square or rectangular shaped projects.

Projects:
One repeat of the pattern uses 42 threads in each direction and consists of the first 42 threads charted within the corner of the design. Suggested projects include a headboard for a bed, a jacket for a large book or scrapbook, pillows, or a tote bag. Use the border alone for mirror or picture frames or repeat the stripes and arrowheads over and over again to create another all-over pattern to coordinate with projects made from the full chart.

Materials:
A 16 mesh or finer gauge in mono interlock canvas is suggested. Use Persian-type wool yarn plus a #5 size pearl cotton or a 6-strand embroidery floss for half of the weaving stitch used in the center of the white crosses.

Needlepoint Stitches:
Milanese
Mosaic
Straight
Tent—Basketweave
Upright Gobelin

Weaving (formed diagonally in two types of white yarn)

Work Order:
Start at the upper left corner and proceed horizontally across the canvas working repeats of the white crosses and the large green paths and crowns. Fill in the smaller details after each row repeat of the pattern. Work the border last.

| | white | | rusty red | | yellow | | green | | light brown | | dark brown |

Oriental Bouquets
Intermediate Skill Level

The drawing of the bouquet and border given here makes it as easy for you to work the design in embroidery on fabric as on canvas. If worked on canvas, you can fill in the background with stitches or not, according to the effect desired. Selecting all the shades of yarn from one color family lends another Oriental quality to the design.

Projects:
The complete design including border is 14" square worked on fabric or on canvas. Arrange multiples of the design together for an embroidered tablecloth or a quilt top. Use single repeats of the design for placemats or pillows and add eyelet ruffles inserted with narrow navy ribbon around the edge.

Materials:
For fabric embroidered projects select a tablecloth or hardanger linen or a medium-weight cotton such as hopsacking that has a distinctive evenweave.

For canvas projects select 16 mesh regular mono canvas if the background is to be left unstitched and a mono interlock if it is being filled in with stitches.

For fabric or canvas projects a size #3 pearl cotton yarn will produce silk-like embroidery. For cotton or linen fabrics linen floss can be used. For canvas only, tapestry or Persian-type wool yarn can be used.

Stitches for Canvas or Fabric:
When the stitches are made on fabric you will have to judge just how close to make them for the desired coverage. It is not necessary that the stitches conceal the fabric as well as is usually needed on canvas. However, do work the stitches at regularly spaced intervals, following the grain of the fabric for the top and bottom of the stitches, just as in working them on canvas.

Brick (horizontal, outside border for fabric or canvas) (optional—horizontal, inside border for canvas work only)

Chain (to outline large and medium flowers) (stems filled with chain stitch on fabric work only)

Cross (berries plus butterfly body on fabric only)

French Knot (flower centers plus head of butterfly on fabric only)

Straight (flower centers plus butterfly body accents)

Slanted Encroaching Gobelin: (to fill in flowers and berries)

>   Small flowers—border, over three threads in pale blue.
>   Medium flowers—over 4 threads, alternate pale and light blue on rows.
>   Large flowers—over 6 threads, alternate medium and dark blue on rows.
>   Berries—over 3 threads, one yarn color per berry as coded.
>   Round flower—over 4 threads, alternate medium and dark blue on rows.

Stem (to outline small flowers, berries, round flower and butterfly)

Tent Continental (stems and butterfly on canvas work only)

Work Order:
Trace the design onto tracing paper, including the entire border. Place this drawing under the fabric or canvas and with a fine tip blue permanent ink marking pen draw the design onto the fabric or canvas. If necessary, use a light box or tape the fabric and paper to a clean window.

Fill in the center of all the design areas according to the stitch and colors required. Then work all of the outlining stitches, chain or stem. Add the freehand embroidery stitches to the top of the embroidered flowers, berries and butterfly. Last, fill in the dark navy outside the border and the white background, if desired, on canvas work.

pale blue   light blue   medium blue   dark blue   white   navy

Birds and Flowers
Intermediate Skill Level

This design has a nostalgic quality reminiscent of the 20's or 30's, particularly when embroidered in cross stitch. The design can take on a soft dimension if the background area between the birds and flowers and the border is quilted.

The design can also be worked in needlepoint with tent stitches. Depending on the use of the design, you may find it more practical to work the white area outside the blue border in dark brown or spruce colored yarn, or to stop the design at the blue border.

Projects:

Worked on 11 to the inch even-weave Aida fabric the design would measure approximately 19" by 15"; on size 14 it would be approximately 14" by 12". Make a serving tray by inserting the design into an antique frame and adding brass handles to the ends. Or, make a quilted tote bag, pillow or picture.

Materials:

For embroidery select white, very pale blue or beige Aida fabric. Select yarn according to the use of the project. On fabric use either a linen floss, 6-strand cotton floss or one strand of Persian-type wool-yarn. For needlepoint, use Persian-type wool to work all the areas except for shiny pearl cotton colors in the flowers.

Stitches For Embroidery:
Cross
Straight (background)

Stitches For Needlepoint:
Cross or Tent—Continental and Basketweave
Straight (on top of background stitches)

Work Order:

Work the central motif of birds and flowers first and then the border. If you plan to quilt the project, remove the work from the hoop when central motif is complete and add a layer of quilt batting and a backing fabric to the wrong side of the embroidery; baste the three layers together. Then work the straight background stitches to form the quilting. Otherwise, make the straight stitches on the single layer of fabric.

If the design is worked on canvas add background stitches to fill in the area between the worked center and border. The straight stitches are then worked as embroidery on top of the needlepoint.

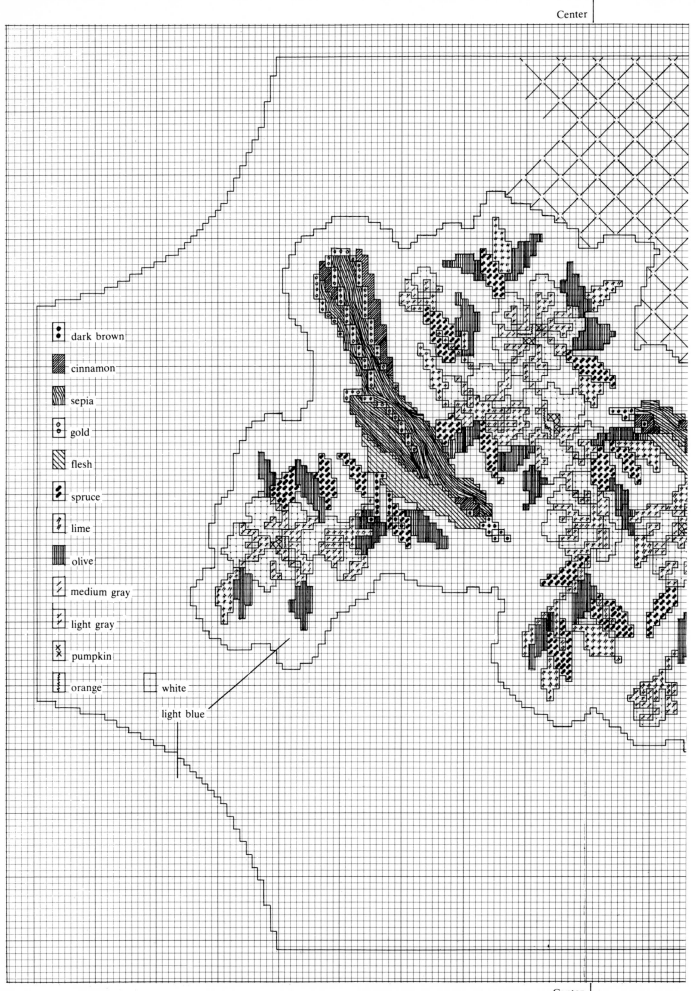

Center

dark brown

cinnamon

sepia

gold

flesh

spruce

lime

olive

medium gray

light gray

pumpkin

orange

white

light blue

Center

Fancy Dresden Plate
Advanced Skill Level

When this design was first made by quilters, the wedge-shaped sections were cut from discarded neck ties of luxurious silks and brocades. Our needlepoint stitch patterns and yarn suggestions are reminiscent of these fine fabrics. See it photographed on page 3. The embroidery stitches worked on the tops of sections one and three lend contrasting textural highlights to the surface of the needlework.

The design can be made even more exciting for the advanced needleworker by mixing the mediums of needlepoint and appliqué. For example, every third section could be filled in with delicate fabric appliqués. In this interpretation all of the needlepoint would be worked and blocked before making a pattern tracing of the open canvas sections to be filled with fabric appliqués. (See page 71 for instructions.)

Projects:

Worked on 16 mesh canvas the design would measure 14½" on each side (and 20" diagonally from opposite corners). A 4½" diameter circle is allowed at the center.

For a pillow, work the design as charted or substitute an initial for the mosaic blocks in the center. The design can also become a mat for a mirror or a picture. Omit the stitches within the center circle and finish the circle with a row of stem stitches before trimming unworked canvas to a ½" seam allowance. Clip, turn, and tack the unworked canvas to the wrong side of needlework with sewing thread. Or omit the center stitches and include names and date for a wedding or birth sampler.

Materials:

To imitate the appearance of silk, choose pearl cotton yarn and accent with yarn for the surface embroidery . . . or use real silk on a petit point canvas.

Use Persian-type or tapestry yarns plus metallic pearl or silk yarns for a more traditional appearance. For the finished piece on page 3

we used the following yarns and threads on 16 penelope canvas:

DMC 3-ply Persian wool, "Floralia":
(using 1 strand unless noted)
Color 7157: magenta—4 yds. (1 skein) (Use 2 strands.)
Color 7799: gray blue—8 yds. (2 skeins)
Color 7357: rust—8 yds. (2 skeins)
Color 7743: gold—4 yds. (1 skein)
Color 7606: Chinese red—4 yds. (1 skein) (Use 2 strands.)
Color 7314: blue—8 yds. (2 skeins)
Color 7072: light gray—6 yds. (2 skeins). Add 1 skein if center is to be worked.
Color 7754: mint green—9 yds. (2 skeins) (Use 2 strands)
Color 7804: rose—6 yds. (2 skeins)
Color 7370: fern green—9 yds. (2 skeins) (Use 2 strands)
White—4 yds. (1 skein). Add 3 skeins if center is to be worked. Use 2 strands for center.
Color 7133: antique pink—11 yds. (3 skeins). Add 1 skein if center is to be worked.
Color 7745: pale yellow—10 yds. (2 skeins)
Color 7257: plum—75 yds. (20 skeins) (Use 2 strands for encroaching gobelin.)
DMC Pearl Cotton Embroidery Thread Size 3:
White—12 yds. (1 skein)
Color 725: yellow—4 yds. (1 skein)
DMC Gold thread: "Fil D'or á Broder",
Size 10—4 yds. (1 spool)
DMC Silver thread: "Fil D'Argent á Broder, Size 10—8 yds. (1 spool)

Needlepoint Stitches:
A bargello pattern
Leaf
Hungarian Ground
Mosaic (background)
Diagonal Mosaic
Oriental
Slanting Encroaching Gobelin (background)
Stem (mirror or picture opening only)
Tent—Basketweave
Weaving
Turkey Knot (pillow fringe)

Embroidery Stitches Over Needlepoint:
French Knot
Chain
Straight

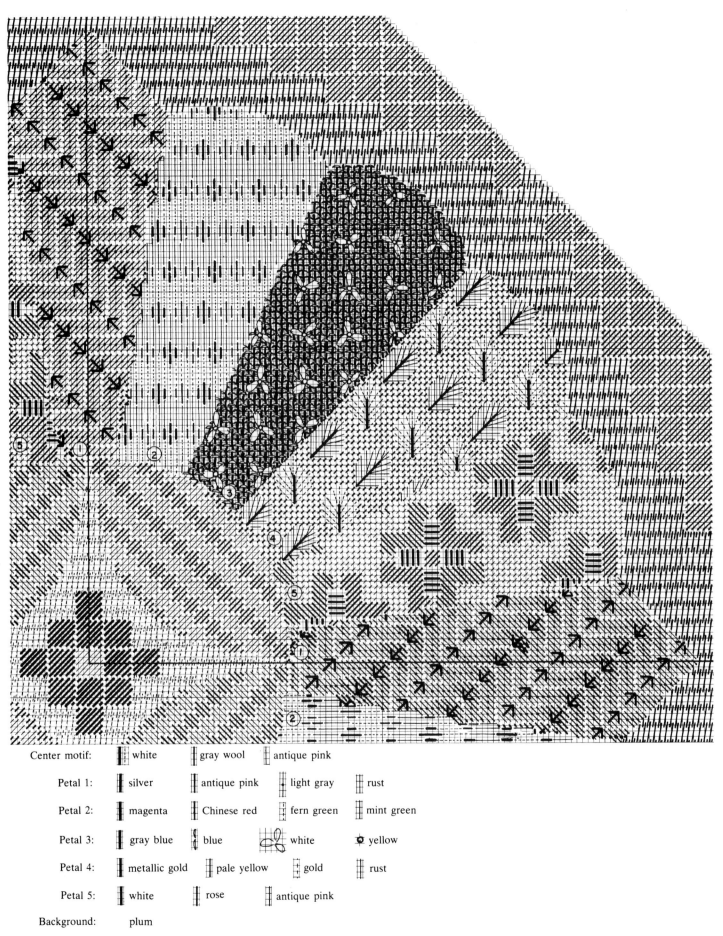

Center motif: ▮ white   ▮ gray wool   ▮ antique pink

Petal 1: ▮ silver   ▮ antique pink   ▮ light gray   ▮ rust

Petal 2: ▮ magenta   ▮ Chinese red   ▮ fern green   ▮ mint green

Petal 3: ▮ gray blue   ▮ blue   ✿ white   ✿ yellow

Petal 4: ▮ metallic gold   ▮ pale yellow   ▮ gold   ▮ rust

Petal 5: ▮ white   ▮ rose   ▮ antique pink

Background: plum

Work Order:

If the project you have chosen includes working the center section of the design, then start there. Otherwise, work the wedge-shaped sections first, then the background. Work the embroidery stitches last, along with the stem stitch around any center opening. Block the finished piece before cutting away all but ½" of the unworked circle for the mat opening.

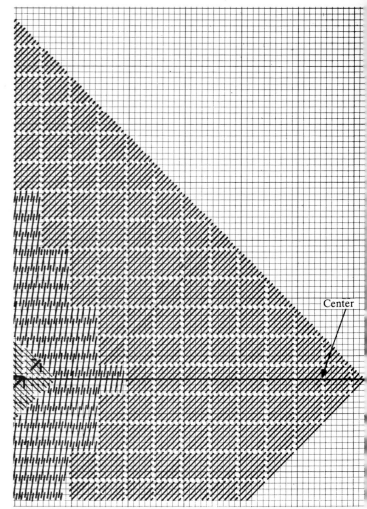

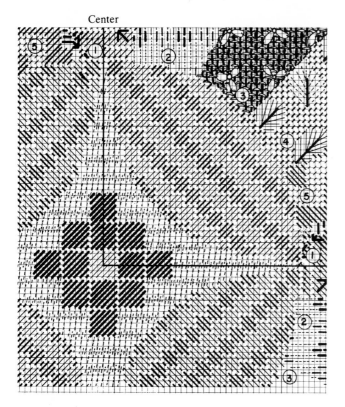

Mrs. Feathersome
Intermediate Skill Level

This strutting hen really comes to life when rick-rack and lace are added to her cross-stitched or needlepointed features. For an even stronger dimensional quality, you can appliqué and quilt gingham fabric sections to the project, then surround her with feather-like background stitches.

Projects:

Mrs. Feathersome could become a cross-stitched friend on a little girl's pinafore, and she is cheerful company on a square pillow or a shaped pillow-toy.

If your canvas or even-weave fabric produces 14 stitches to the inch, a square pillow would measure 12" and a shaped pillow-toy would measure 6¾" by 10".

Materials:

To cross stitch the design, use an even-weave fabric such as Aida or hardanger cloth. Or, the body features can be cross-stitched on a small-scaled gingham fabric. Mark the perimeter of the gingham dress with a light pencil and trim around the hen leaving a seam allowance so that she can be appliquéd to another fabric.

The entire design may be worked in needle-point or, if you wish, the apron or background tent stitches may be omitted if a regular mono (non-interlock) canvas is used.

Select yarns appropriate to the use and care of the project. Couch red baby rick-rack around the outer edge of the comb and right and left sleeve, along the hem of the dress and around the cheek. Add a ½" wide lace edging to the hem of the apron.

To finish pillows, tack large rick-rack around the outer edge.

Needlepoint Stitches:
Leaf (elongated; background)
Mosaic
Diagonal Mosaic
Tent—Continental and Basketweave (background)
Chain (pillow-toy only)

Alternative Stitches:
Cross
Double Cross
Upright Cross

Work Order

Start with the head and work down, then fill in the background border and filling stitches. Finish and block a needlepoint project before applying any trims. If rick-rack is desired around the pillow, sew pillow first and then tack the trim to the seam before stuffing. For the pillow-toy finish off the perimeter of hen with chain stitch before sewing and stuffing.

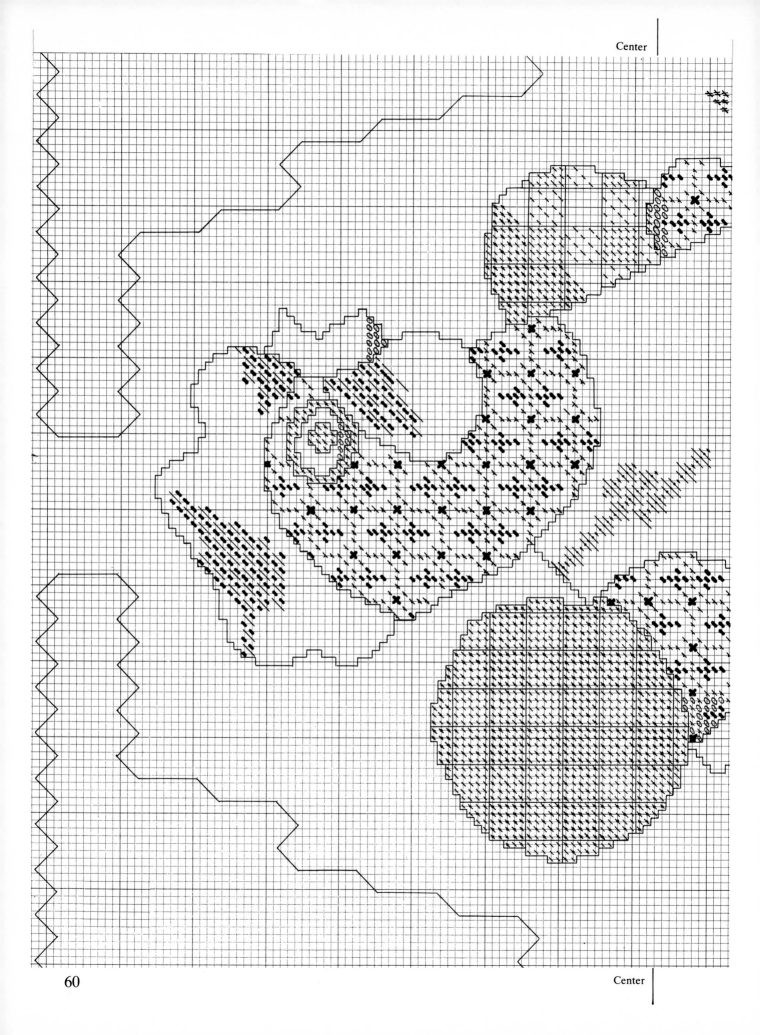

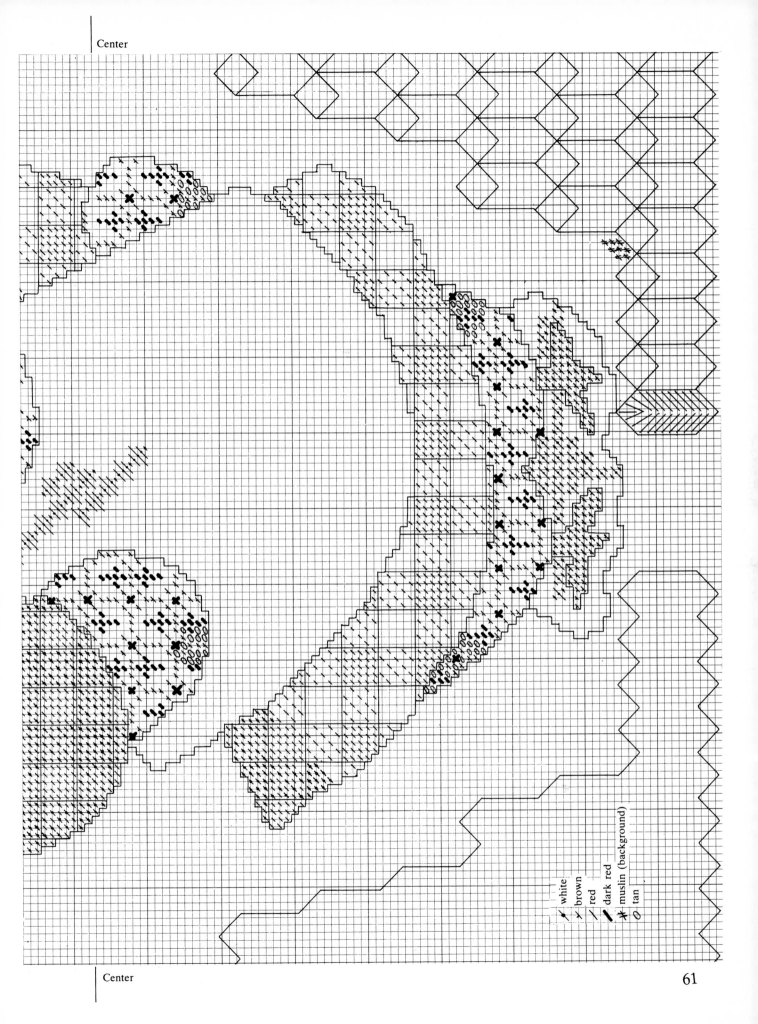

Grandma's Favorite
Intermediate Skill Level

Grandma's favorite will become yours too if you enjoy making the lovely lacy patterns of pulled thread embroidery.

The two simple stitches worked in your choice of one or two colors of an interesting yarn can keep repeating themselves to any size for projects on either canvas or even-weave fabric.

Projects:

One repeat of this design spans a width of 48 threads by a depth of 38 threads and includes two V-shaped rows of upright crosses and a central eyelet pattern. Additional upright cross and eyelet stitches form the border.

The pattern is a natural for table linens—tablecloth, placemats, runners and napkins. Or, for a new experience, work pulled-thread embroidery on a fine canvas for pillows, using the canvas just as you would a fabric.

Materials:

Select even-weave fabrics of cotton or linen such as hopsacking, Cork linen or hardanger fabric. Linen floss is a perfect companion for these fabrics and so is cotton floss and pearl cotton. For canvas pulled thread work you must work on a regular mono canvas, not one of interlock construction, and preferably in a fine gauge of about 18 mesh. Use any of the above yarns or silk buttonhole twist. In any case, yarn used for pulled thread embroidery must be strong with a high twist like the suggested types.

Stitches:
Eyelet
Upright Cross

Work Order:

Work a complete upright cross or eyelet stitch before proceeding to the next stitch, tugging the yarn after each insertion of the needle so that the fabric or canvas becomes distorted and its threads are pulled toward the center of the stitch. The tugging or pulling causes the separation in the threads in the fabric which forms the lacy look in the finished pulled thread embroidery.

Work the design in horizontal rows of the repeat. Work the border last from the center to the corner on each side.

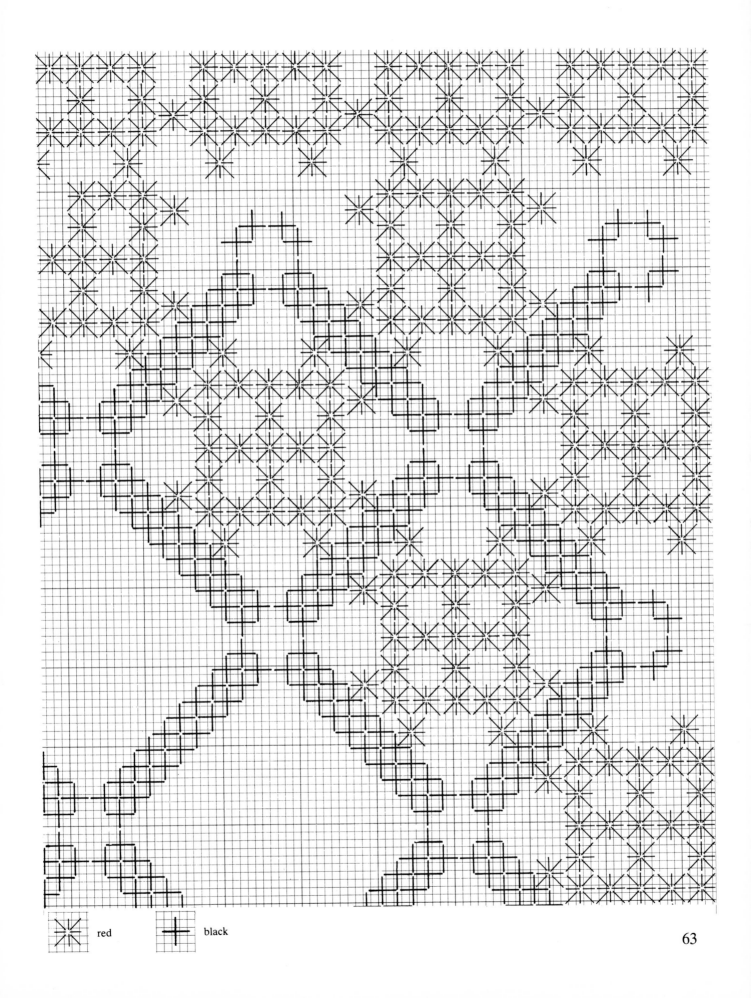

red   black

George Washington's Cherry Tree
Advanced Skill Level

For the cover of our book, this needlepoint project was worked life size to the quilt details. On page 4, it is shown finished as a large stacked floor pillow. The needlepoint stitch patterns and color variations add an interesting contrast to the coordinated projects. A contrasting pale yellow yarn worked in straight stitches between the blocks of the background imitate the yellow quilting stitches on the original quilt.

Projects:

As photographed, the design makes a 32" square floor pillow using 12 mesh canvas. If you prefer smaller pillow projects, make a diamond shaped one using just the tree section of the design with only one green stripe around it for a border. The corner motif of the cherries and leaves can be made as a triangular pillow, with or without a single green stripe border. A narrow red border can be added around the outside of either of these similar pillows.

If you want to turn George's tree into your own family tree, embroider family names around the sides inside the outer white border. Write or print the names on tracing paper to fit the space. Then embroider them in chain stitch through the paper and the surface of the needlepoint stitches and remove the paper when finished.

Materials:

We used Persian-type wool for all the stitches except for the pearl cotton mock quilting stitches on top of the mosaic background.

Needlepoint Stitches:
Encroaching Upright Gobelin
Upright Gobelin
Hungarian Ground
Mosaic (background)
Upright Cross

Embroidery Stitches Over Needlepoint
Straight (background)
Chain (optional, for names)

Work Order:

Thread baste the vertical and horizontal center lines of the design on the canvas. Count out 145 meshes in each direction from the center and mark by basting between these points to establish the inner line of the inside border. Work the inner and outer green borders first, then the tree, leaves, cherries, and the corner motifs. Finish by working the mosaic background (counting the blocks from the center in all four directions). Work the white and red borders and then add embroidery stitches.

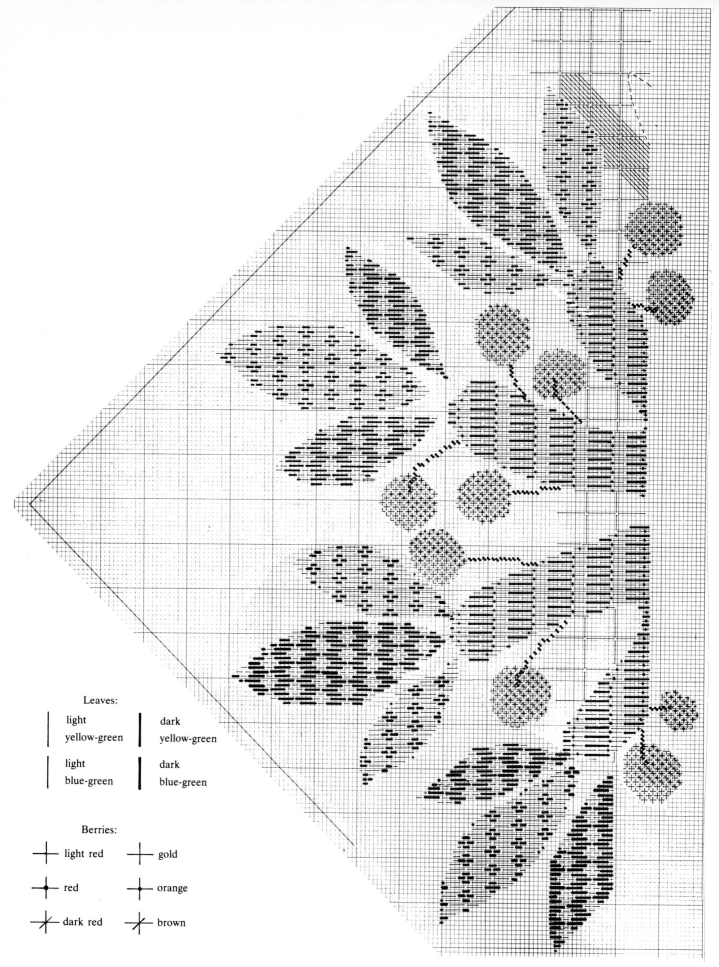

Leaves:

light
yellow-green

dark
yellow-green

light
blue-green

dark
blue-green

Berries:

light red

gold

red

orange

dark red

brown

66

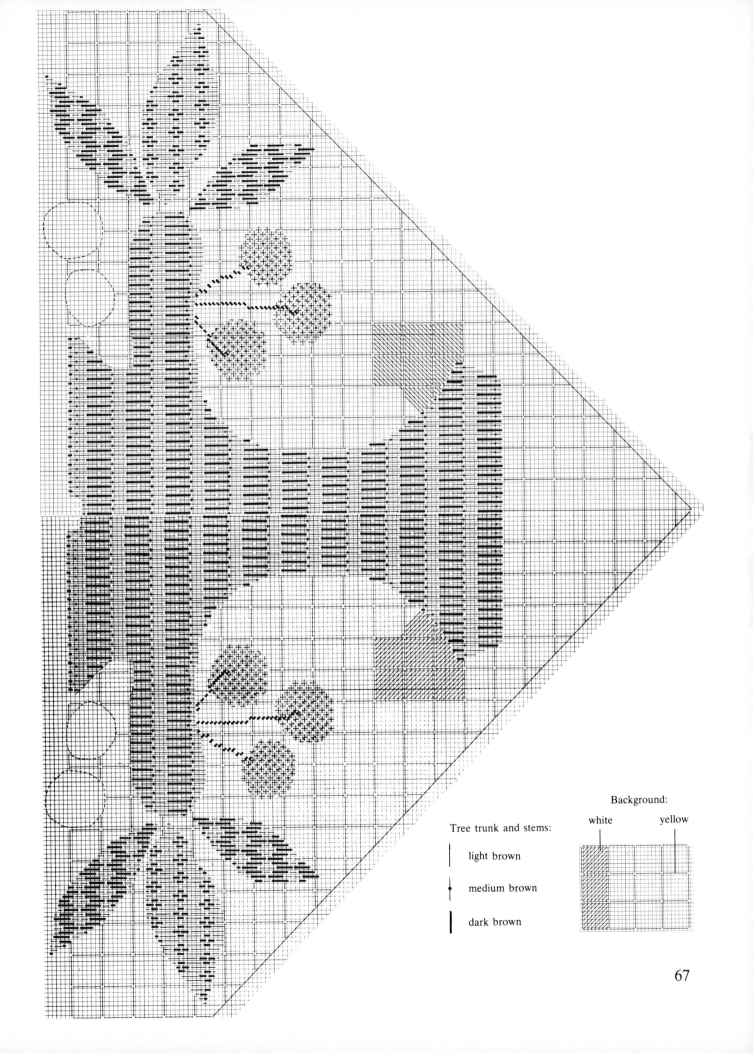

Tree trunk and stems:

| light brown

•| medium brown

| dark brown

Background:

white   yellow

67

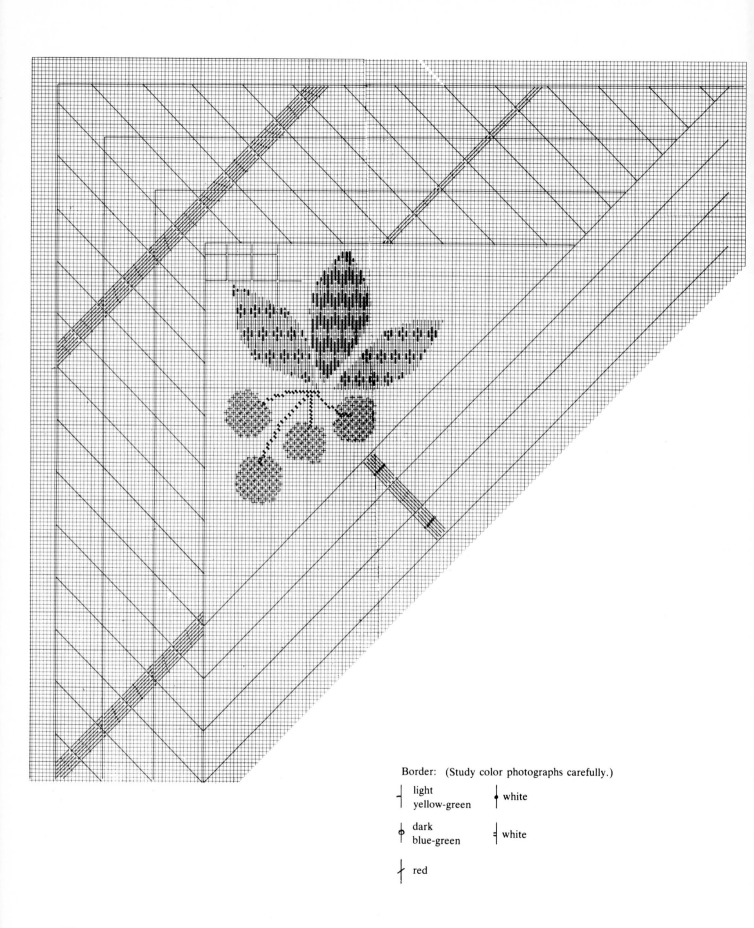

Border: (Study color photographs carefully.)

† light yellow-green   ● white

φ dark blue-green   ⌇ white

⨍ red

68

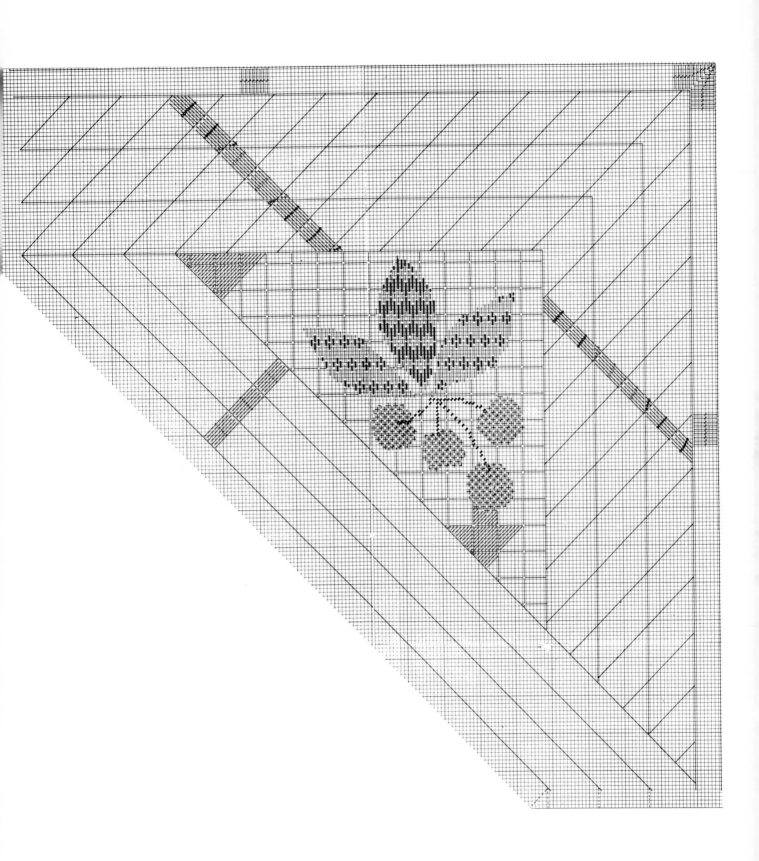

69

General Instructions for Working from a Charted Design

The most important thing to remember in working with a charted design is that *each intersection on the graph represents one stitch.*

To determine the size of a finished piece that will be worked by following a graph, count the squares in the height and width of the design. No matter how many squares there are in an inch on the graph, the design can be stitched on a canvas or fabric of any mesh you choose. (Mesh is the number of stitches allowed for in an inch of fabric or canvas.) A design charted on twelve squares to the inch graph paper may be stitched on ten mesh needlepoint canvas, 22 mesh petit point canvas, 14 mesh Aida cloth, 5 mesh quick point canvas, or any other mesh canvas or cloth that you want to use. The fact that the chart shows twelve squares in an inch does not affect the size of the finished work . . . the number of stitches that you work in an inch determines the finished size.

Mathematics can be irritating when you are anxious to begin stitching, but it is necessary. If you do not figure carefully at the outset, you may find that you have bought much more material than you needed, or, much worse, that your stitches run off the edge of the material. In this case, the whole piece will have to be discarded and begun again. Here is a useful formula:

The number of squares in the height of the graphed design

divided by

the number of stitches in an inch of your needlework

equals

the number of inches high the stitched design will be.

The same formula works for determining the width.

When you know how long and how wide your stitched design will be, you must then allow extra material around the edges for whatever you wish for background, plus 1 to 1½ inches for finishing.

Example: A charted design counts 120 squares high by 84 squares wide. To work in needlepoint on 12 mesh canvas, divide 120 by 12 and 84 by 12. The design will work out to be 10 inches high and 7 inches wide. If you want 1 additional inch of background stitches all around, the finished piece will measure 9 by 12 inches. Add 1½ inches for finishing; you will need a piece of canvas that measures 12 by 15 inches.

To work the same design in cross stitch on 22 mesh hardanger cloth, divide 120 by 22 and 84 by 22. Your answer will be 5.45 inches high and 3.8 inches wide. Round off the figures to 5½ by 4 inches. If you want an additional ½ inch all around for background material, the finished piece will measure approximately 6½ by 5 inches. Add 1½ inches all around for finishing and you know you will need a piece of hardanger cloth that measures 9½ by 8 inches.

Work from the center out. Begin counting at the center of the chart and stitching at the center of the material. Usually it is easier to work up from the center and complete the upper part of the design, then finish the lower part. However, it may be easier to outline a central figure, beginning with, or close to, the center stitch, then work to fill in the upper portions of the design, followed by the lower portions.

Find the middle of the chart by counting the number of squares up the height and the number of squares across the width. The place where the exact center of these lines cross each other is the center of the chart. Mark this center point on the chart.

Find the center of your canvas or cloth by folding it in half lengthwise, then again crosswise. Mark the center of the canvas or cloth. The safest method is with a sewing thread that can be snipped out after the work is begun. If you use a pencil, use it lightly.

The center of the chart may fall on one square of the design, or it may be somewhere in the background stitches. The center of the *chart* is not the same as the center of the *design*. You will, however, begin stitching from the center of the design. Work stitches, after the first stitch, to the right, left, or up, counting squares on the chart and working stitches in the same places on the canvas or cloth.

General Instructions for Adding Fabric Appliqués to Needlepoint Projects

This procedure is also applicable to other needlework projects such as cross stitch or embroidery.

1. Complete all the needlepoint areas and block the project.
2. Place the area to be appliquéd over a piece of paper backed with cardboard and secure with push pins. With a separate push pin, punch through the canvas and paper around the perimeter of the area to be appliquéd, making prick marks on the paper.
3. Remove the canvas and sure-up the prick marks by drawing over them with the aid of a ruler or a French curve. Cut out the paper pattern.
4. Use this pattern to cut a layer of fleece-type interfacing or one or more layers of cotton flannel so that the interfacing plus the appliqué fabric is equal to the thickness of the stitches above the canvas.
5. Cut out the appliqué fabric 3/8" larger all around than the interfacing.
6. Baste the interfacing and fabric layers together and then baste the fabric edges to the wrong side.
7. Place the appliqué over the unworked canvas area and stitch it in place with sewing thread along the edge of the needlepoint stitches.
8. If appropriate to the design, add quilting or embroidery stitches to the appliquéd section.

The Stitches

The stitch dictionary on pages 74–78 illustrates stitches that are drawn on a grid which represents needlepoint canvas. These stitches are made the same way when they are used on linen, gingham, or any other type of material for regular embroidery.

Stitches on canvas can be divided into three very broad categories . . . tent stitches, florentine stitches, and bargello stitches.

A *Tent stitch* is any stitch which covers one thread intersection on the top of the canvas and two thread intersections underneath. There are several versions of the tent stitch: the most often-used ones are the basketweave and the continental. The half cross stitch is not a true tent stitch in that it covers one thread intersection on the top of the canvas and only one intersection underneath. It is useful in changing the direction of the stitching—for example, if you want to change from stitching from left to

right to working down.

Study Figure 1 to learn how to follow any stitch diagram. Bring the needle up from underneath the canvas on odd numbers (1, 3, 5), and put the needle through from above on even numbers (2, 4, 6). The lighter stitches represent half cross stitches.

The basketweave stitch, also known as the diagonal tent stitch, should be used for backgrounds and any design areas that have many stitches of the same color (Figure 2). After the first three stitches, the rows in black are worked diagonally down, with the needle put through the canvas vertically. Rows of stitches drawn in gray are to be worked diagonally up, putting the needle through the canvas horizontally. Remember that the needle comes up from underneath the canvas on the odd numbers and goes in from the front on the even numbers.

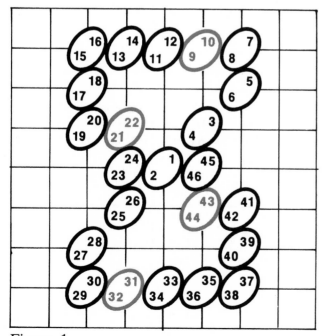

Figure 1

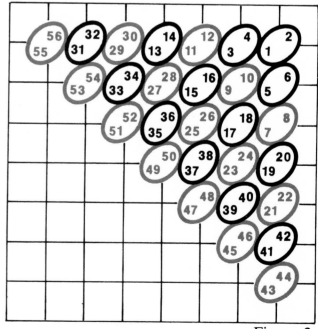

Figure 2

72

The continental stitch is illustrated in Figure 3. "A" shows how to work the stitch from right to left; "B" shows how to work it from left to right. If you work from left to right, use a "stick and stab", rather than "needle through" method. Make sure each row of stitches slants

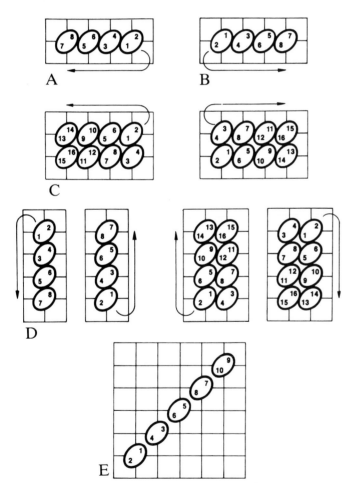

A

B

C

D

E

in the same direction. "C" shows how two rows can be worked at once. "D" illustrates how to work the tent stitch vertically, in single and double rows. To work a single row of tent stitches slanting from lower left to upper right, as shown in "E", use a "stick and stab"

motion, not "needle through".

Florentine stitches are, by definition, those stitches that are always and only formed with and parallel to either the lengthwise or crosswise grain of the canvas threads.

Bargello stitches are, to state it simply, any pattern stitches which do not fall into the Tent or Florentine stitch categories. These stitches are most often formed diagonally on the canvas, as illustrated by the Mosaic stitch. However, bargello stitches can also be formed of combinations of diagonal and straight stitches within a stitch repeat, as in the Triangle stitch.

Some bargello and Florentine stitches have specific traditional names such as Byzantine or Old Florentine; others do not, because they are specially designed to fit a shape or space within a motif. Therefore, we have used the term Straight Stitch to denote any stitch which has not been traditionally named, no matter whether it is formed parallel to or diagonally on the canvas grid.

Traditionally-named stitches are sometimes known by more than one name. For example, the Eyelet stitch is also known as Algerian Eye, Algerian Star, and Eye stitch. We have selected what we feel is the most commonly used or most descriptive name for each of the pattern stitches without endeavoring to list alternative names.

Also, you will find that the same stitch will be utilized in several variations or in different sizes within a single design. Should a stitch within a charted design vary slightly from the dictionary version, use the dictionary only as an explanation of the movement of the stitch for the purpose of learning how to form the stitch. Follow the specifics on the designs to get length or count of the stitch necessary for working the project.

Stitch Dictionary

Alternating Scotch Stitch

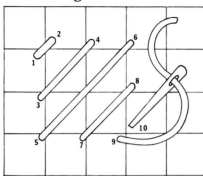

In progress

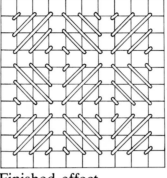

Finished effect

Back Stitch

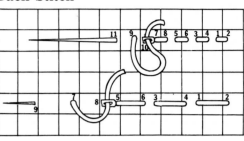

Binding Stitch

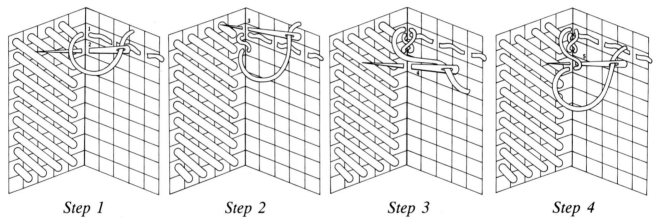

Step 1 *Step 2* *Step 3* *Step 4*

Brick Stitch

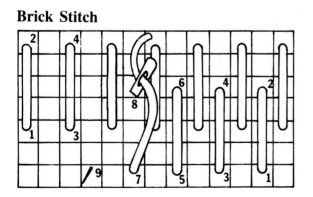

Buttonhole Stitch

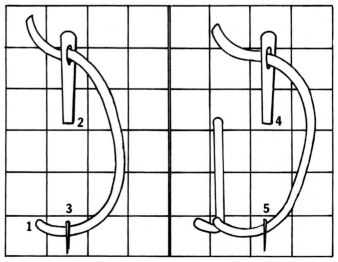

74

Byzantine Stitch

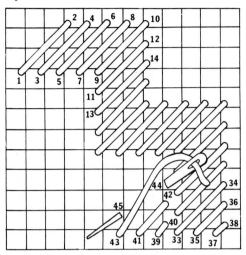

Chain Stitch

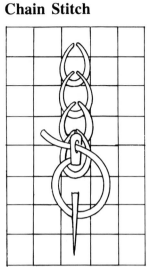

Cross Stitch

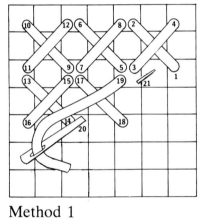

Method 1

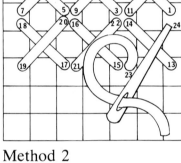

Method 2

Diagonal Mosaic

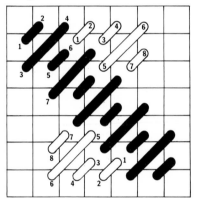

Double Cross Stitch

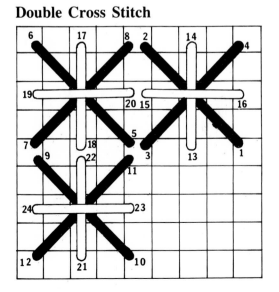

Encroaching Gobelin

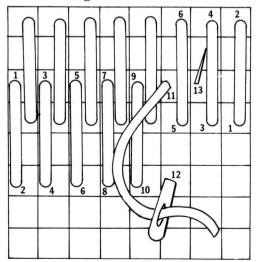

Eyelet Stitch

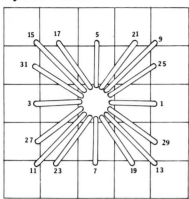

Eyelet Stitch (variation)

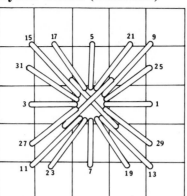

French Knot

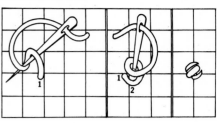

Hungarian Ground Stitch

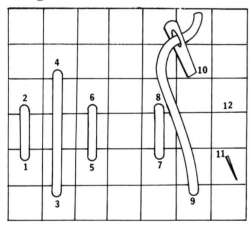

Leaf Stitch

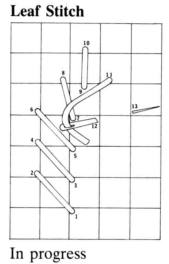

In progress

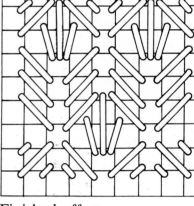

Finished effect

Milanese Stitch

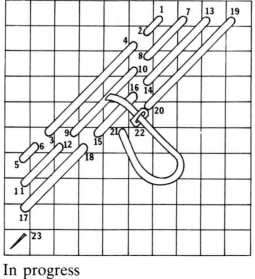

In progress

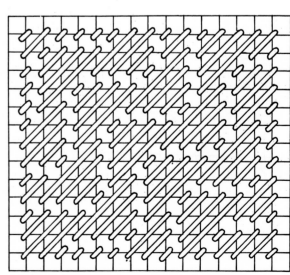

Finished effect

76

Mosaic Stitch

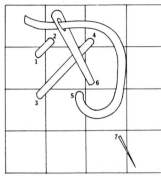

In progress

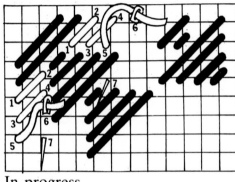

Finished effect

Stem Stitch

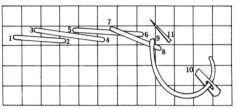

Oriental Stitch

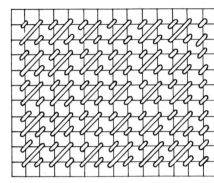

In progress

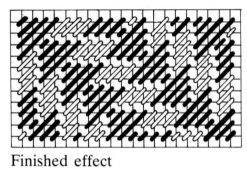

Finished effect

Slanted Encroaching Gobelin

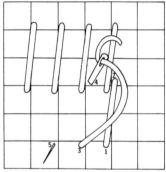

Straight Gobelin Stitch

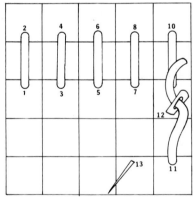

Triangle Stitch

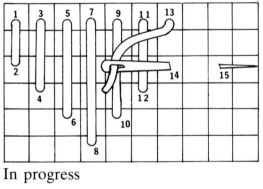

In progress

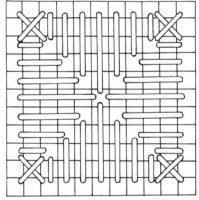

Finished effect

Turkey Knot

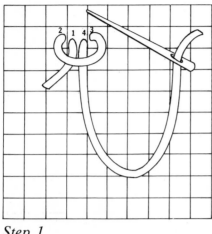

Step 1

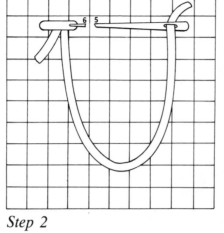

Step 2

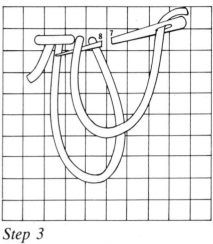

Step 3

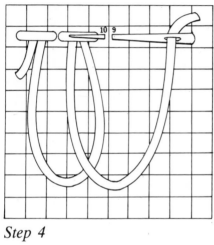

Step 4

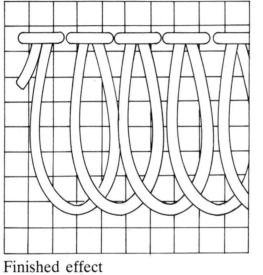

Finished effect

Upright Cross Stitch

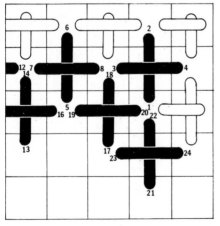

Woven Stitch

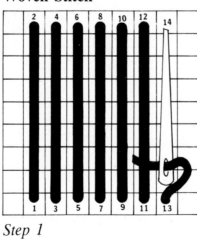

Step 1

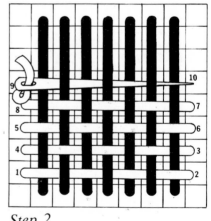

Step 2

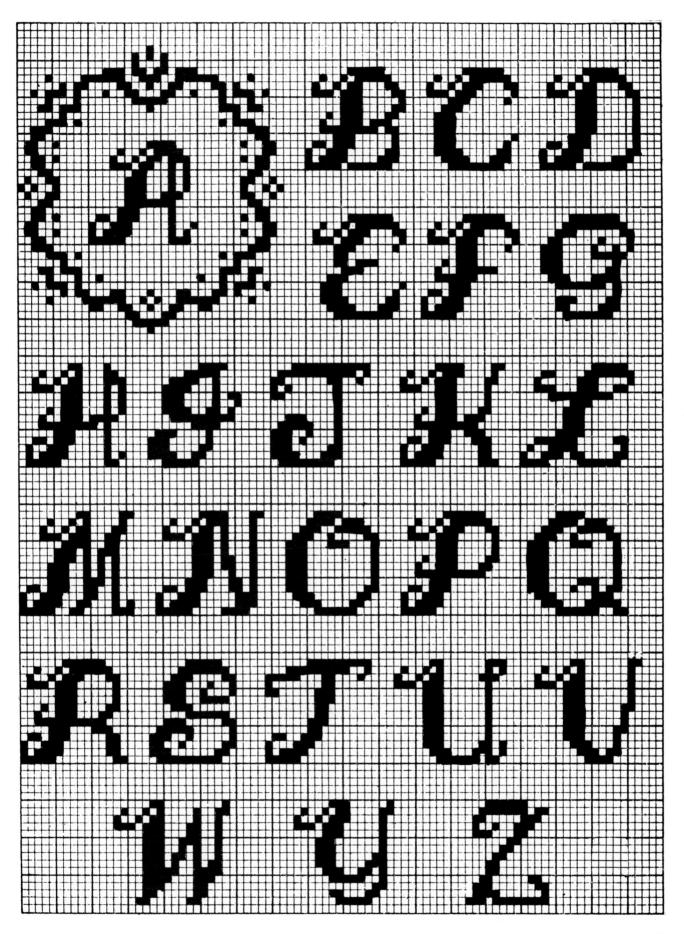